THE ILLUMINATION CODEX
GATEWAY FOUR

Chakra Yoga Discourse

Keys for Higher Consciousness

Michael Garber

MICHAEL GARBER

Printed in the United States of America
First Printing 2021
First Edition 2021

Second Edition

ISBNs:
Softcover 978-1-959561-13-2
eBook 978-1-959561-14-9

10 9 8 7 6 5 4 3 2 1

The
Illumination
Codex

Table of Contents

ACKNOWLEDGMENTS

I bow in humble recognition of the One Light of Consciousness, the Source of my being and the source of all knowledge and wisdom. I give gratitude to the Supreme for dreaming me into existence and allowing me to have the conscious experience of life and the crafting of this codex.

I bow in love and gratitude to my dear beloved partner Ron Amit, a true gift of the Divine, for all the many ways he supports me in my life. I am blessed beyond measure to have such a brilliant master of love, compassion, and divine service to walk this earthly life with. Thank you for all that you do, seen and unseen, to amplify joy and higher consciousness for me and all beings in the Cosmos. I love you across all space, time, and dimensions.

I send gratitude to my friends and clients who have brought forth the lost stories of Creation through their Illuminated Quantum Healing hypnosis sessions. Thank you for being the powerful Light beacons that you are!

I send deep gratitude to my many modern scribes who assisted me in the transcription work. Thank you for helping me capture these incredible client stories so that the world can remember our cosmic divine heritage.

Bless all the beings, seen and unseen, who have helped me craft this material so that you, the reader, can be nourished on your path of Ascension. May you, the reader, be blessed infinitely and discover the highest truth of your being. May ascended consciousness, liberation, and divine unification be yours in this very life!

DEDICATION AND INVOCATION

This book is dedicated to the infinite expressions of our Oneself, for the celebration of our many incarnations, past, present, and future, and the lessons we have learned throughout eternity. May these words and the energy they carry be a potent force for awakening for all seekers of Unconditional Love and divine Truth. May this transmission support the reactivation and restoration of humanity's divine blueprint upon planet Earth and accelerate the realization of our eternal unity and oneness with all of Creation.

Let us join in prayer, honoring and sending gratitude to the Supreme Intelligent Source of Creation, the omniscient, omnipotent, omnipresent, transcendental Divine Source that is our True Nature.

Let us honor and send gratitude to the higher Light realms and the beings of Light who guide and protect Creation's evolution. Let us honor and send gratitude to our star lineages and those who support us from beyond the Earth. Let us receive your love and blessings now as we remember our cosmic ancestry and our role in the higher evolutionary plan for Creation.

Let us honor and send gratitude to our Earth Mother and her many dimensions and manifestations of Life including the animal, plant, bacterial, fungal, protozoan, mineral, crystalline, and elemental beings who contribute to her dynamic, regenerative biomes. These writings are offered as salve and balm to heal and bless our beloved Gaia, our Earth Mother and Divine Sister. May her waters be pure, her soil rich, her air clean, and may all beings, seen and unseen, within her living biofield know lasting peace forever and ever.

Let us honor and send gratitude to the wisdom and guidance from the seven directions of East, South, West, North, Above, Below, and Within. Let us call back our soul fragments scattered through time and space so that we may anchor ourselves HERE and NOW in this eternal moment of infinite potential to witness the unfolding manifestation of the Divine Plan.

Let us honor and send gratitude to the elements of Earth, Air, Fire, Water, and Ether that create the foundation of our evolutionary experience in form. May the Light of Consciousness awaken swiftly in each of us as we remember our True Nature beyond names and forms.

Let us honor and send gratitude to our ancestors and the many souls who have shared their light upon the Earth. Let us send special thanks to those who dedicated their lives to passing on the Mysteries and sacred knowledge of the Divine so that we may NOW stand at this Grand Turning of the Ages, with the support of all who have come and all who are destined to live upon this great Earth.

I call forth the full remembering of our divinity and the weaving of a new story of harmony and peace for all of Life upon the Earth. May we shed our stories of limitation and suffering and step forward into a new era as People of Light, cosmic co-citizens, and ambassadors for the Living Light of Creation.

Hallelujah! Jai! Aho! Blessed Be! Amen! And so, it is! Om!

GUIDANCE FOR READING THIS BOOK

The Illumination Codex is a multidimensional library for the path of Ascension. It is holographic by nature as each chapter contains a multitude of keycodes to activate ancient cellular memory and trigger multidimensional awareness and higher consciousness integration. As you read the material, your Inner Being will offer flashes of insight and higher perception into your awareness to assist you in healing, spiritual activation, and cosmic remembrance. I recommend using a highlighter, journaling your process, and using other resources to research and enhance your understanding of the topics presented in this book.

A major influence for this material comes from my work as a past-life regression hypnotherapist using the methods we have codified into a technique called Illuminated Quantum Healing (IQH). While in a deep hypnotic trance, my clients experience other lifetimes and other planetary civilizations and communicate with advanced intelligent species from beyond the Earth and Earth plane. The information contained in this book is a summary of my understanding of all that I have learned through my clients as they journeyed to the ancient past, probable timelines of the future, and higher planes of Light. There are many transcriptions of IQH sessions included in the book for you to have your own unique interpretation and multidimensional experience with the material.

This book contains a diverse collection of spiritual information from a variety of wisdom traditions that I have studied in my life. These writings are my own interpretations and understandings of these different concepts that have helped me in my awakening journey and do not necessarily speak for the lineages themselves. This presentation of information is meant as a collection of keys to unlock the wisdom that is already encoded within you. None of it is meant to become dogmatic as consciousness revelation and ascendency will open us continuously to higher and higher truths and understanding.

I confess that I share this transmission as a fellow traveler on the path of awakening. I have my own limitations, my own egoic nature, and my own struggles. I am capable of error and ignorance just as any other person. This presentation of information is what I have found along my path which has triggered awakening and helped me on my path back home to my Self. My prayer is that this book will become deeply meaningful for you and be a guiding light back to your own liberated being.

While reading this material, you may come across something in the text that triggers something within you that is uncomfortable. Maybe it is words that I use, perspectives that I share, or something else that may bring up resistance, judgment, anger, guilt, and so on. This is a wonderful opportunity to investigate the origin of the reactive mental and emotional patterns that create such experiences. The origin may come from earlier stages of your life or previous lifetimes. Use this as an opportunity to reconcile those parts of your consciousness through spiritual inquiry and self-study so that you may realize deeper states of wholeness and clarity.

This text is intended to activate 'gnosis,' a direct experience and knowledge of the divine presence within and around you. I do not recommend blind faith in any concept or religious doctrine. The information in this book is not meant to be treated as religious dogma that cannot be questioned or developed further. It is meant to be utilized to unlock the truth that lives within your very being. I am not writing this intending to change people's beliefs or convert anyone. I am simply relaying the summary of my life's research on the quest for spiritual truth. If something from the material does not resonate as truth in your heart, release it and move on to the next part of the transmission. Use the philosophy and information in this text to stimulate your expansion and the embodiment of YOUR deepest truth and to strengthen your relationship and innate connection with the Divine.

Another thing to mention is capitalization. You will notice that there are words that are not normally capitalized in other books and sacred texts that are capitalized in this text. My intention behind this was to add spiritual dimensionality to words that describe qualities or names of the Divine.

Typically, when I speak of light in this book, I am speaking about higher-dimensional, intelligently-encoded subtle energy and not conventional light from a light bulb. When I speak about "energy," I am speaking about subtle energy which exists beyond the visible light spectrum for most people. Many are becoming sensitive to subtle energy (i.e., multisensory, intuitive, psychic) and are developing the ability to sense and perceive this energy through extrasensory perception. All of humanity is evolving towards being able to perceive and interact with subtle energy and higher cosmic intelligence and consciousness.

The use of the term consciousness fluctuates throughout the book and can mean different things. When I speak of pure Consciousness I am speaking about your True Self as Source Consciousness, the Absolute, the Eternal Witness of all Creation, pure Awareness and Existence itself. Other times I will speak of consciousness as in variations of the mind such as unity consciousness or separation consciousness. All forms of consciousness, all experiences of the mind, borrow existence from the One Light of Consciousness and you are that!

I tried my best to organize this text in a way that can be read from front to back like any regular book, but it can also be read any way you feel intuitively called to read it. Part of the reason for the size of this codex is because it is difficult to explain one part without understanding many other components. In my effort to answer all potential and probable questions about ascension, I wrote everything I could on this multifaceted, multidimensional topic.

As you make your journey through this material, there are three stages to help integrate the information and use it to fuel your awakening to your True Nature:

Stage One: Listening (*Sravana*) As you read or listen to the material in this book, allow it to penetrate deeply and work with your inner philosophical understanding. Listen deeply to your Inner Being for there will be flashes of insight and knowing that emerge within your inner consciousness space.

Stage Two: Reflection (*Manana*) Try your best to understand the information contained in this book through self-inquiry and inner philosophical pondering. I am not asking for you to blindly believe any of this transmission. Think of this information as an active hypothesis. You do not have to believe it, but you can reflect over the information and see how it applies to your life.

Stage Three: Integration/Meditation (*Nididhyasana*) As you take in the words in stage one and convert the words to knowledge and understanding in stage two, you move into conviction and integration of knowledge in stage three as you crystallize and embody the Self-knowledge of "I am Pure Consciousness." As you go about your daily life, use the knowledge you have gained to interrupt habit and conditioned thought and re-direct your mind toward the Light of Consciousness that you are.

Gateways of Entry

Besides reading front-to-back or intuitively hopping around, I have created six gateways for you to enter the presentation of the material. I have created one large book that has all of the Illumination Codex material and separated the material into separately published volumes to make the information more digestible. The Gateways are as follows:

GATEWAY ONE: ASCENSION INITIATION: KEYS FOR HIGHER EVOLUTION gives an overall understanding of Ascension, reincarnation, universal law, and a theoretical and philosophical framework concerning Cosmic Evolution. This is an excellent place to start if you are open and eager to learn about these subjects and awakening, you may want to start in Gateway Three.

GATEWAY TWO: AKASHIC DATABASE contains a wide variety of Illuminated Quantum Healing session transcriptions describing key figures and events in the history of Creation, galactic history, ancient planetary history, and probable future timelines of New Earth from clients in hypnotic visionary states. This is a suitable place to enter the material if you already have a general understanding of multidimensionality, galactic civilizations, and the process of personal and planetary ascension. This gateway is conveniently separated into QUANTUM ORIGINS, COSMIC CHRIST TRANSMISSIONS, and NEW EARTH TRANSMISSIONS. If you find yourself resistant to those ideas and are new to these subjects. I recommend developing a meditation practice parallel to reading this material as the transcripts are deeply activating on multiple levels.

GATEWAY THREE: PATH OF AWAKENING: KEYS FOR TRANSFIGURATION is an in-depth collection of spiritual and philosophical wisdom to support personal, relational, and planetary healing. If you are in the beginning stages of awakening or moving through a deep healing process, you may wish to start here so you can develop your consciousness and prepare your mind and body for higher level initiation into the Mysteries.

GATEWAY FOUR: CHAKRA YOGA DISCOURSE transmits deeper

insight into the themes and physio-psycho-spiritual domains of the vortices of life force and perception called the *chakras*. Each section transmits valuable information to understand the common distortions in these processing centers and how to activate and reconcile each center.

GATEWAY FIVE: LAYING HANDS: REIKI & BEYOND is a full manual for learning the art of the laying of hands for healing. The manual clearly describes all the stages, steps, and practices to perform powerfully transformative hands-on-healing sessions for yourself, others, and even in groups. This manual would be acceptable for any Level 1 and Level 2 Reiki course.

GATEWAY SIX: ASCENSION LEXICON is a glossary of commonly used words to describe the process of awakening and ascension. These definitions act as keycode activators to unlock deeper meaning and inner wisdom. Many words used in spiritual/ascension circles are convoluted and sometimes lose their impact because they are misused or misunderstood. I may use words in a way you are not familiar with, or I may use words differently than you. I tried my best to make a glossary with foundational vocabulary to assist with understanding the material. You may wish to read the ASCENSION LEXICON before journeying through the main text of the book.

Bless you on your personal path through this material. May the light in your heart guide you with ease and grace on your journey of initiation with *The Illumination Codex*.

ABOUT THE AUTHOR
Awakening to the Quantum Reality

In the Summer of 2016, I was given a book that forever changed my life's direction called *The Three Waves of Volunteers and the New Earth* by Dolores Cannon. This book was a huge catalyst in my spiritual awakening. Reading the text stirred something deep within me and resonated profoundly with my heart's truth. The book's pages sent waves of energy down my spine as I began to awaken to a higher consciousness reality and remember my purpose for being born upon the Earth at this time.

Dolores Cannon was a world-renowned hypnotherapist specializing in past-life regression. To understand the power of regressive hypnosis, we also need to understand the workings of the mind. The mind can be separated into three categories: the conscious mind, the subconscious mind, and the superconscious mind.

The conscious mind is the ego/personality part of the mind. This active part of the mind uses limited information from the environment and past experiences to make decisions and take care of the body.

The subconscious mind is the recording device of our mind. It records incredible amounts of information at every moment. We easily pull data from the subconscious when we think about something from our past as we access memory.

Deeper in the subconscious, sometimes called the unconscious mind, we have unconscious memories and information, including societal conditioning, painful traumas from this life that are too painful to remember, and memories from other lifetimes. Even though this information is not in the conscious mind, it silently influences our day-to-day experience as reactive emotional momentum, called *samskaras* in Sanskrit, from past events which overlay and filter our experience of the present moment. These subconscious patterns are like applications running in the background of smartphones that quietly drain the processing speed and battery, silently influencing processor speed and functionality.

The superconscious mind is a higher mind capacity that gives us access to intuitive information, extrasensory perception, non-local consciousness, creative genius, universal connection, and access to divine consciousness. This part of the mind is mostly undiscovered and underdeveloped in most of humanity.

Dolores created a unique method of hypnosis, Quantum Healing Hypnosis Technique (QHHT), that opened a doorway to the client's subconscious mind to explore other lifetimes and realms in Creation. When I use the word "quantum," I am speaking to the fabric of Consciousness, the multidimensional unified field of Creation. When clients are in these hypnotic states, they tap into the part of their consciousness that is nonlocal and connected to All That Is. This includes access to other lifetimes, other realities and dimensions, and other intelligent consciousness forms (i.e., higher-dimensional light beings, telepathic extraterrestrials, etc.). Through this experience, clients came to understand another perspective and origin of self-sabotaging and limiting beliefs that were playing out in this life and the core mental/emotional patterns that create illness and disease.

During her sessions, Dolores started to contact a part of her clients' consciousness that seemed to have endless knowledge and wisdom. She called this aspect of her clients the Subconscious or the SC. Others have called this the Higher Self, the oversoul, superconsciousness, or the cosmic consciousness. I prefer the term Higher Self and superconscious mind and go into great detail of how to activate and evolve superconsciousness throughout this text. While the information was limitless, the SC/Higher Self would only answer questions in a way that was appropriate for the client's learning path and honored their free will. When working with the SC, both Dolores and the client described powerful healing energy in their bodies and the treatment room. Clients often reported instantaneous healing as they were transformed from the inside out during the session. While this may seem too good to be true, there are countless documented and measurable occurrences where clients received lasting miraculous healing through these types of sessions.

When she would work with the Higher Self, this higher consciousness identity and supportive Light team would speak through the client as a collective consciousness as if the client were speaking in third-person perspective about themselves. "We are always guiding her. We wish she would follow her intuition more." and "We are beginning to use white light to heal this now." are common examples of how "They" (i.e., SC/Higher Self) express themselves and heal the client during the session.

The healing work is always done with unconditional love and honors the free will and sovereignty of the client. If instantaneous healing was not "appropriate" for the client's growth and spiritual maturation, "They" would suggest what steps the client should take to heal themself. Slowly, over many years, Dolores's work expanded as "They" introduced more components to the healing process so that she could evolve her work and teach it to others.

The Three Waves of Volunteers and the New Earth was one of nineteen books written by Dolores Cannon before her transition out of physical life. Each book contains transcriptions of client sessions describing detailed events from other lives while using her Quantum Healing Hypnosis Technique (QHHT).

Awakening to the Starseed Volunteer Mission

After several years of working with clients worldwide, Dolores noticed a pattern of clients describing a massive galactic and higher dimensional mission to raise the vibration of the planet and shift it into a new reality called the New Earth. The book describes how countless numbers of advanced spiritual beings from distant star systems, and even other universes, volunteered to incarnate on the Earth with a mission to raise consciousness on the planet and assist with this grand transition.

The New Earth is a higher frequency Earth reality that exists in a higher dimension than we are in now. Clients describe a large-scale plan initiated by Source Intelligence (God) to reset life on planet Earth back to the original template of a harmonic environment thriving within diversity. Parallel to this, Dolores's work described a shift in human consciousness from a duality-based mindset to a heart-centered, multidimensional consciousness and a less physical body of light.

The First Wave Volunteers were born beginning around 1945 through the 1970s. They were like a stealthy reconnaissance mission. First on the scene. First to patrol and feel out the collective consciousness vibrations. First to introduce the higher consciousness perspectives to the masses. Many had a difficult and lonely time since there were not many other humans in higher, love-based spiritual consciousness on the planet at the time.

The Second Wave Volunteers were born around the late 1970s through

1990s and are channels for higher spiritual energy and divine wisdom. These souls came in with a higher level of intuitive gifts and are often extremely sensitive to energy. Many are hands-on healers, musicians, vocalists, yoga teachers, and so on. They are space-holders who transmit a new frequency out to the field of Earth, bridging the old ways with the new ways and consciousness of New Earth.

The Third Wave Volunteers, the younger generations, are builders and innovative geniuses in science, spirituality, technology, and so on. They are divinely inspired visionaries that will build the New Earth. They are radical lovers and shine bright with crystalline eyes and have achieved high consciousness levels in other lifetimes. Some of these souls have never had a physical incarnation or have come straight from Source as new souls with pure Light and no karma.

I have been told all the children born at this time are part of this Grand Mission. They are pure souls, evolutionary masters, here to build the New Earth. More is written about the Starseed Mission and phenomena later in this book.

As I was reading Dolores's book, I felt I was reading my own story. I felt the truth in her words. Suddenly so many things made sense about my life. I finally had answers to why I felt so different from others in my community and family. I understood why I felt other people's emotions and could tell what people were thinking. It all started to click together. I was so excited to share the book with Ron, my husband and co-founder of New Earth Ascending, who also deeply resonated with the material.

At the same time, we were beginning to work with an Australian musical group as dancers for their "Return of the Bird Tribes" tour for their album by the same name. Something about the term "bird tribes" caught my attention, and I started to research it. I found the book by the same name, written by Ken Carey, in 1988 that describes a prophecy of high spiritual beings returning to the Earth at a time of spiritual renewal.

Many cultures describe times when culture-bringing beings would come from the heavens or from across the waters to bring technology and information to humanity throughout history. Thoth went to the Egyptians, White Buffalo Calf Woman went to the Native Americans, Quetzalcoatl went to the Aztecs, the Seven Sisters of the Pleiades went to the Aboriginal people of Australia, beings from the Sirius A and B binary star system went to the Dogon people of Mali; and many other stories exist in many other cultures. Carey's book described when these beings would come again during a time of spiritual awakening on the planet.

I was receiving information from multiple directions and was going through a massive realignment with my soul's purpose as I became aware of this greater story and mission. Ron and I went to an arts festival in the desert of Nevada called Burning Man. While we were there, a couple excitedly recognized us as "twin flames" and asked us which star system we had come from. "We are from Sirius. Where are you from? Orion? The Pleiades? Sirius?" she asked. The concept of "starseeds" and "twin flames" was new to me, and I did not know what to say. I saw a special sparkle in the couple's eyes and felt that I should do some research to understand more about it.

After some research and some magical synchronicities, Ron convinced me that we should do the QHHT training and certification process. I was super resistant to learning it because of deep religious programming and egoic structures that made me doubtful of the truthfulness of the work. I was familiar with reincarnation but did not necessarily believe in it. Eventually, I gave in to Ron's suggestion and took the QHHT course.

Evolving Beyond QHHT

In the early stages of practicing QHHT, Ron and I were guided to start doing the sessions online to share the technique's power with as many people as we could. This method was not permitted by the organization because Dolores did not believe it to be safe and her organization does not permit it still. Dolores was an elder and this type of technology was new to her, whereas the younger generations are much more comfortable interfacing with video conferencing.

We have been told by the Higher Consciousness that there is nothing to fear, and NOW is the time to spread these healing methods across the world in whatever way is possible. To honor our lineage and teacher, we stopped using the name QHHT and started experimenting with different names as our way of practicing quantum healing evolved beyond our initial training.

Online sessions are just as powerful as in-person sessions and are often more comfortable and affordable for the client. It is completely safe to facilitate sessions remotely, and we have had countless powerful sessions that have been facilitated in this way. Dolores's organization does not allow adaptation of the QHHT technique. Its practitioners need to perform the method exactly how Dolores taught and not add any modifications or outside techniques. While it is important to protect the work's integrity, this rigidity does not permit the work to expand to its full potential. We are in a time of expansion and evolution, and we must always be open to the transformation and progression of all methods we currently use or risk leaving them in the past as everything on the Earth is evolving.

Another topic that caused us to evolve beyond our initial training of QHHT was the organization's strict denial of negative spiritual attachment and what felt like shaming those who believed in this common experience. Ron and I and other quantum healing practitioners discovered that certain psychological, emotional, and physical imbalances were being created by pervasive energies that did not belong to the client's energy field that had somehow become attached to the client. This includes spirit attachments, curses from past lives, and implants from nefarious beings to name a few. QHHT did not provide us with appropriate training to work with these serious complications. If it were found out that a practitioner had adopted these practices and still operated under the name of QHHT, practitioners could be removed from the QHHT directory.

Many practitioners have reported spontaneous visitation from Dolores through clients under hypnosis where she has encouraged practitioners to follow their intuitive guidance and continue to develop the work through experimentation just as she did when she developed QHHT.

We were inspired greatly by other quantum healing practitioners' extraction methods and crafted our own approaches to clearing pervasive energies and spirit attachments. The reality of negative thought-forms, negative extraterrestrial implants, and entity attachment is too big to ignore, considering so many cases are emerging, not to forget the thousands of years of wisdom and extraction practices passed down by Indigenous peoples and various wisdom traditions.

We never assume that someone has an entity just because they suffer, and we do not bring it up in our intake interview. Once the client is deep in a hypnotic trance, we ask the Higher Self if there are entities or attached energies. If the answer is yes, then we ask questions to understand how this occurred and if the client has anything to learn to release negative attachment. From there, the Higher Self can immediately extract the energy and take it back into the Light for healing. It is all extremely safe, insightful, and benefits all who are involved. We have found that, often, the revelation of spirit attachment or implants will not occur unless the practitioner asks and gives permission for a scan specifically for attached energies. Ron and I believe this is because of the honoring of the free will of the entities involved in the experience of attachment.

In my opinion, to continue to deny such experiences is a disservice to the clients who come to us seeking answers and healing. All practices and traditions can become dogmatic if we do not allow the evolution of thought to take us into new frontiers of consciousness. These are evolutionary practices, and we need to be constantly open to shifting our paradigm so that we can offer the best guidance and support with the changing of times.

Once we started offering quantum healing sessions online, clients started coming to Ron and me from all over the world. Not only were the sessions powerfully healing and transformative for the clients, but we were also going through a rapid transformation as we learned about ancient stories and galactic events from the perspective of souls embodied at those times. While Dolores taught that many people had "potato-picking lives," simple lives with simple themes, it seemed that almost every session of mine had to do with the New Earth Mission, powerful events from the ancient past, and future timelines of Earth.

I soon realized that I was getting a theme and timeline in my sessions. The timeline given to me via my clients describes how Creation came into being, ancient galactic history, the seeding of life on Earth, the rise and fall of ancient civilizations, the true teachings of Jesus through the eyes of people that were closest to him, information about the transformation of the human body to a less dense body of Light, and the evolution of the Earth into the higher frequency reality of New Earth. In less than a year, I went from a reincarnation skeptic to believing that anything is possible, and that the multiverse is more incredible than we can even imagine!

Illuminated Quantum Healing

After years of practicing and evolving how we do this work, Ron and I have created our own quantum healing method that incorporates all that we have learned on our path. This includes facilitating sessions online to reach as many people as possible to assist in this Great Awakening.

Our training method acknowledges spirit attachment and teaches our facilitators how to perform negative spirit releasement. We teach yogic psychology, holistic wellness concepts, and energy healing methods to ensure the practitioner has a thorough understanding of human consciousness and how to lead the client through the ascension process using multiple IQH sessions and mentorship programs. We call our method Illuminated Quantum Healing. IQH can be learned in live classes or through our online course offered on our social network Source⊙Energy.

Illuminated Quantum Healing (IQH) is a personal transformation method for multidimensional holistic healing and consciousness development. IQH incorporates energy healing, meditative practices, yogic philosophy, and hypnosis skills to reconcile limiting subconscious patterning and integrate instantaneous multidimensional healing and wisdom from one's Higher Self.

I am deeply honored to be a part of this work. I am so blessed to have an opportunity to work with such incredible people and energies. Each session that I facilitate nourishes me to the core, and I have the sublime opportunity to observe miraculous instantaneous healing and transformation in my clients. After witnessing the infinite potential of quantum healing hypnosis, I firmly believe that we can ascend beyond all states of illness and disease and that we have infinite support to move beyond the shadows of our past and become a new People of Light.

Getting to the New Earth involves a process of spiritual growth and purification. To transition with the Earth, it is required that we raise our vibration to match the accelerating frequency of the Earth as it changes. Mostly, this is about releasing fear and negative karma. I have written this book as a tool to use for your spiritual awakening and transformation that many are calling Ascension. This is my gift to humanity to help make the process easier and explain different components to cultivate a deeper understanding of this Grand Shift to New Earth and our newly evolving Lightbody.

Spiritual awakening and ascension are available for ALL people no matter what they have done in their past, current economic status, gender expression, sexuality, religion, etc. There are as many paths to the New Earth as there are humans on the planet. No one religion holds the keys or the way to heaven. The power is within YOU!

To support the global ascension process, we have created New Earth Ascending. New Earth Ascending is a non-profit, faith-based organization focused on global ascension and establishing heart-centered, sustainable communities and educational centers around the world.

Alongside Illuminated Quantum Healing (IQH), Ron and I have created other pathways of support for the global ascension process:

1. Embodied Light Reiki Training and Certification
2. New Earth Ascending has three levels of Reiki certification to train people how to channel divine light for healing. These trainings honor the lineage and teachings of the Usui System of Natural Healing while also infusing evolutionary concepts and practices that go beyond standard Reiki training.
3. Online courses for awakening and ascension are available on our private social network Source⊙Energy. The courses include philosophical exploration on several models of spiritual growth and alchemical practices to support your healing, awakening, and ascension. These courses include meditations, holistic wellness education, breathwork, lightbody activation and more. These courses lay foundational understanding for beginners and move through a progression of intermediate and advanced practices and knowledge.
4. TransformOtion was created to support the embodiment of one's Higher Self using dance, somatic movement, yogic practices, meditation, imagination, and energy healing. This fusion of practices helps to purify and repair the physical, etheric, and mental bodies so that one can move beyond perceived limitations into boundless rhythm and flow. Through this interweaving of multiple disciplinary paths, we integrate physicality with transcendental ecstatic play while cultivating a deep connection with and trust in the body's wisdom.

   These ideas and concepts can be used for personal embodiment and activation or infused into performance art to create powerful alchemical experiences for the performer and the audience. This fusion of high art and spiritual transformation creates a multidimensional experience for all who are within the field of performance energies.

5. Source⊙Energy is a social network exclusively for those on the path of ascension to connect and share inspiration as we manifest and build a New Earth. We invite all souls who feel aligned with New Earth to join this network and add your unique energy and love to this community. Source⊙Energy serves as a pathway of social interaction and is the home of our online courses and training.

6. Children are our future. Youth inspiration and enrichment programming is in development to assist the spiritual activation and consciousness mastery of the youth. NEA is dedicated to creating harmonic environments and rich educational programs to guide youth to connect with cosmic intelligence and embody their divine nature and mastery as they build the New Earth.

Ron and I have dedicated our lives to supporting this Grand Transition. We stand alongside all of you as humanity awakens to its True Nature and becomes a People of Light in the heavenly reality of New Earth.

New Earth Ascending is dedicated to assisting people to realize their divinity and manifest that truth in every aspect of their life. For more information about New Earth Ascending or to contact Michael, please scan the QR code below for a list of resources and links, or visit *www.newearthascending.org*. Be sure to check out our courses including the Illuminated Quantum Healing practitioner course.

New Earth Ascending is a registered 508 (c)(1)(a) Self-Supported Non-profit Church Ministry with a global outreach. We greatly appreciate your support as we create new systems, communities, and schools for the development of the New Earth civilization. If you would like to make a tax-deductible donation to support our mission, please go to:

https://donorbox.org/donationtonewearthascending

Scan with a smart device camera for more information!

NEW EARTH ASCENDING
VISIONARY CREED

We acknowledge the sovereignty and equality of all levels of Creation and support the liberation of all of Life from cycles of suffering. We believe in the power of divine sovereign creatorship endowed to us by God/Source and dedicate our life to Light and Love in service to All. We believe in conscious participation, empowering everyone to activate awakening in themselves and their community.

We recognize free will and surrender our will and desires to the higher will of the Divine. We believe in divine timing and practice trust, patience, and tolerance as we witness the unfoldment of the perfection of the Divine Plan. We believe in the potency of empowering prayer, meditation, and ritual as tools for communication with the Divine for the culmination of spiritual light and divine wisdom. We believe everyone has a direct connection to the Source and no intermediary is needed. When we come together in fellowship, prayer, and devotion, we amplify the light of each individuals' loving intention through our unified, heart-centered consciousness.

We seek to uplift all groups and communities so that we may celebrate our unity, diversity, and wholeness. New Earth Ascending is non-competitive and embraces an ecumenical relationship with all religions and wisdom traditions. We believe in interfaith and inter-spirituality, acknowledging the teachings of Light, Love, and Wisdom in many traditions, philosophies, and cultures. We believe that no single religion holds the keys to the Kingdom of God and the blessings of redemption are available to all people through their unbreakable innate connection to the Godhead.

We believe in the Law of Oneness and that all of Creation emanates from one Divine Source that has both masculine and feminine principles. As we heal and balance the divine masculine and divine feminine principles within us, we embody the divine androgyny of Source and Nature as a harmonic synthesis of Spirit and Matter.

We believe that humanity and planet Earth are going through a rapid physical and spiritual transformation called by many as The Ascension or The Event. We believe this process to be part of a higher evolutionary divine plan guided by the Source of Creation and legions of beings working for the Light. This evolutionary process is multidimensional and is beyond the standard biological evolution spoken of by modern science.

We believe that we, as humanity, are awakening to our spiritual Self and are becoming a heart-based, unity-focused species with higher, multidimensional awareness, which some call Christ Consciousness, Cosmic Consciousness, or 5D Consciousness. We believe this transformation's power is happening through our divinely designed and curated DNA as the physical body transforms into a less dense body of Light with tremendously expanded multidimensional abilities.

We believe that Planet Earth, the sentient being of Gaia, is going through a similar restoration process and will soon transform into a revitalized higher dimensional planet, which many are calling the New Earth. Earth changes, weather events, crumbling institutional structures, frequency fluctuations, and astrological phenomena are all signs that we are nearing that shift into the next Golden Age, where Heaven and Earth become one and all systems of control and limitation will fall away.

We believe that we are supported by benevolent higher dimensional, subterranean, and extraterrestrial beings that work in harmonic collaboration with the higher evolutionary Divine Plan of Source. We believe that soon humanity will be consciously reunited with these benevolent beings and serve the higher evolutionary plan of the Light and Love of Source as cosmic co-citizens of the Multiverse working as one Family of Light in service to all of Creation.

We understand that the pathway of Self/Source-Realization and Ascension is comprised of self-study, self-practice, self-discipline, and steadfastness. We practice self-care and self-purification to clarify our Light. We acknowledge and value the acceleration of this process when we practice together in groupings of two or more in fellowship and worship.

We strive to grow in awareness and focused attention, practicing mindfulness in all areas of our lives to grow as conscious, heart-centered creators. We choose to focus our life positively with faith and knowing that Life is evolving in perfection following the Divine Plan of the Supreme Source.

We believe in the power of intention. We practice nonviolence and non-harmfulness in intention, thought, and action. We strive to release all forms of judgment and dual thinking. We honor the sacred heart's radiant potential and believe loving compassion and understanding to be The Way. We practice the heart-centered qualities of gentleness, reverence, loving-kindness, and forgiveness as pathways to reconciliation to emulate the eternal grace of Source and our Earth Mother, Gaia.

We see that Truth is alive within each of us, and we practice inner reflection to grow in discernment for what energies are resonant with our inner Source and our path. We practice benevolent truthfulness, honesty, straightforwardness, and vulnerability to embody and vocalize our deepest truth.

We value and practice transparency and accountability, believing in the opportunity for spiritual growth through spiritual partnership with our community members. We recognize one another as divine mirrors, reflecting to us where we are in our vibration, beliefs, and intentions.

We practice sacred sexuality as an alchemical tool for Divine Union and Ascension. We strive to purify our intentions and desires to align with Higher Love and authentic connection. We believe in heart-based self and consensual mutual pleasure to unite body, mind, and spirit so that we may deepen in our love and authentic connection to our Divine Self, our partner(s), and Creation.

We practice contentment, acceptance, appreciation, and gratitude for our life's many blessings and lessons. We practice non-attachment, non-possessiveness, non-stealing, non-excess, and sustainability, for all we need is given to us through our alignment with our Creator Source and our connection to our Earth Mother. We practice stewardship and sustainable selfless service, acknowledging our responsibility to take care of the world around us and within.

We practice sacred commerce, investing our resources, time, and energy towards the greater good and sustainability of our community and planet. We believe in reciprocal energy exchange and strive to do so when able. We practice generosity, hospitality, and charitability as reflections of the abundance of the Universe.

We strive to embody and emulate these spiritual principles to manifest the complete liberation of all beings from cycles of suffering and to assist this Grand Transition into the New Earth.

Bless us all!

GATEWAY FOUR:
CHAKRA YOGA DISCOURSE

Keys for Higher Consciousness

This section initiates the reader into the deeper psycho-emotional components of the chakra system to reconcile and balance the polarities of each chakra to create coherence and the unification needed for Ascension.

ONE

Pranamaya Kosha: Pranic Body

In the beginning stages of spiritual awakening, we begin to realize that there is something more to physical life than what can be experienced with the physical senses and mainstream reality structure. We begin to sense something mystical to life and begin to turn inward to listen to our inner realm and tune into the interconnectedness of life.

As we awaken, we begin to discover that we exist within a unified field of light and vibration, a continuum of energy that is constantly shifting and changing through an infinite latticework of geometric grid patterns which mesh together to create the holographic matrix of the universe. When I use the word 'energy' throughout this book, subtle energy is what I speak of. Subtle energies are the substratum of all manifestations in Creation and act as the organizing principle, providing the pathways and movements of Consciousness as it evolves within the Unified Field of Creation. Subtle energy is interactive with our own consciousness. As we focus on it, it begins to transform immediately as it links with our consciousness giving us the ability to transfer will and intent across time and space such as in prayer and psychic phenomena.

It should be mentioned that not all energy is "good energy." There are seemingly negative, entropic energies that take away life force, and there are positive, centropic energies that sustain and revitalize life. These energies aren't "good" or "bad" as each frequency serves a purpose or function. The "problem" with energy comes when things are out of sync with Natural Order and are not able to balance and integrate back into wholeness.

In Samkhya, dualistic Vedic philosophy, there is the pure Self, *purusha*, and matter and form, *prakriti*. *Prakriti*, *maya* consists of three fundamental forces: *sattva*, *rajas*, and *tamas*. These forces called *gunas*, translated as "strand" or "fiber," are the threads that weave the web of the manifestation of the cosmos. All phenomena that can be experienced, seen and unseen, is a manifestation of the weaving of the matrix with the force of the *gunas in conjunction with the subtle and gross elements of earth, air, fire, water, and ether (space).*

These forces can be described as follows:

- *sattva*: harmony, purity, light, beauty, balance, consciousness revelation, balance, inspiration
- *rajas*: change, activity, active energy, unsteadiness, movement, agitation, transitions us to sattvic or tamasic
- *tamas*: darkness, conceals consciousness, ignorance, depression, dullness, stagnation, inertia, stability, mindless, intoxicating, inaction

All of these forces can be positive when in balance with the other forces. Ultimately, we should be guiding our experience into sattvic states of balance and inspiration versus the downward spirals that leads to ignorance, decay, and stagnation.

Most ancient cultures have various ways of accessing, manipulating, and understanding the many subtle energy categories and their qualities. There are many names in many cultures for subtle energy. *Ki* (Japanese), *prana* (Sanskrit), *chi* (Chinese), *ruach* (Hebrew), and *life force energy* (English) are just a few.

Prana is the animating life force of the physical body and the active power behind all vital phenomena in the universe. We receive this "breath of life" from the food and water we ingest, our environment, our inhalations of breath, and from our soul and higher consciousness connection. While *prana* is necessary for biological life to exist, too much of it causes nervousness and psychosis and in the most extreme case death. Having too little of it causes exhaustion, and our physical life is over when there is no longer *prana* in the physical body.

Alchemical practices like tantra, yoga, qi gong, and the laying of hands work with subtle energy to restore balance and harmony to a person's physical, vital, and mental bodies to create homeostasis and alignment with one's True Nature. Group prayer and ceremonies create a powerful energy field that amplifies prayers and intentions, and many people experience spontaneous healing and emotional healing through the group prayer field.

Many people who have not had a subtle energy experience of their own find it hard to believe that subtle energy exists, believing in only what they see with their physical eyes. Many reject the idea of a subtle energy reality. Scientific communities are beginning to develop instruments that can measure subtle energy. Many hospitals and clinics in the West are now beginning to allow practitioners of acupuncture and hands-on healing methods like Reiki into the hospital system to support patients' recovery.

Simple Energy Exercise

One of the best tools to sense and interact with subtle energy is with the hands. The awareness is amplified when you apply conscious breathing to the task.

Bring your palms together and begin to rub them vigorously while you consciously breathe in and out of your belly. Close your eyes and feel the sensations. Intend to generate powerful energy and heat. Use your breath and intention to amplify the vibrations, intending for the energy field to grow stronger and brighter. After a few moments, begin to open your hands slowly. Tune into the sensations between your hands. What do you feel? What do you sense? Trust your feelings. Can you feel both the electric and magnetic qualities? Warm or cold sensations? Tingling? This is a form of subtle energy. You can take your hands and lightly move them across your face and body and sense the energy there. When finished, keep the awareness, and open the eyes.

The Human Energy System

Inserted in the physical body and extending slightly beyond is the vital body, also called the etheric body or pranic body. The human body is a multidimensional bio-transducer, meaning it constantly receives, transforms, and emits various levels of subtle energy. The vital energy system translates energy information into the physical systems to create physical body functions like heart rate, hormone release, breathing rate, and beyond. This sheath bridges our physical body with our mental body by translating subtle energy information for physical and mental processes.

In Theosophy, this layer is called the Etheric Body Double because it is similar in shape and size to the physical body. Every cell of the body, every particle of bodily fluids, bodily gas, and organic material is surrounded by an etheric energy envelope that weaves a matrix of pathways to unify all systems. As information streams in through the physical sense experiences, information is passed from the cells into the etheric double of the cells and is translated through subtle information pathways to the etheric brain and mental body. Higher consciousness information and mental patterning experienced in the mental body are transmitted through the etheric pathways and etheric brain into the physical brain and nervous system to direct the body's actions and functions.

Aura: Your Personal Space

All living organisms have an auric field which is called a biofield in science. The human biofield is a toroidal field of electromagnetic light that emanates from the core of your being and creates the matrix framework for your physical body. The aura includes the etheric structuring of the *pranamaya kosha* as well as the oscillation and activities of the mental and causal bodies. Our aura is multilayered and is in constant evolution and transformation based on our mood, thoughts, the food we eat, location, etc. Our auric field is the instrument we use to interact with the subtle energy world around us. It receives energy information from outside of our physical body and radiates energy information into the Unified Field of Creation. Our overall light quotient in our auric field is dependent on the health of all our koshas. Our auric field becomes unstable and distorted when we are in states of aggression, sadness, or other lower emotions. Our auric field is harmoniously organized and coherent when we are in higher vibrational states like joy, creativity, and devotion.

Aura Experience

Close your eyes and begin to focus on your breath and the subtle sensations of your experience. Call the Light to be with you and feel your vibration begin to rise. Imagine that within your heart center, in the core of your being, is a sacred fire, a beautiful bright Light of Source Energy. Use your intention, focus, and breathing to expand this source of energy until it surrounds you. Make your space feel beautiful and loving and filled with light. Deep, full breathing amplifies the radiance and love from this Light. Allow your thoughts to be purified and your mind relaxed by this Light. Feel your intention to merge with the Light and evoke feelings of peace and tranquility. Amplify these positive sensations with your breathing. Notice how far your personal energy field goes. Is it a bubble or does it fade out into the space around you? Feel the energy within you. Notice any stagnant areas, and breathe light and awareness into them, inviting movement and flow.

As you inhale, pull your field back into the core of your being. As you exhale, pulse your light back out. Keep repeating this pattern as if you are flexing your etheric muscles. With each exhale, your aura is brighter, cleaner, and more pronounced. Enjoy this for as long as you desire. When you are complete, feel your aura strong and illuminated. Feel blessed by the experience and open your eyes.

Boundaries

It is important to do frequent aura clearing and restructuring throughout the day, especially if you live a hectic life. Having healthy, energetic boundaries ensures that we do not take on the energy of other people and places. Having a clear aura helps you to have clear thoughts and a joyful mood. Practices like smudging or spraying "aura mists" over the body help to clear and recharge the energy field. It is especially important to intentionally restructure and strengthen your energy field when you go into public so that you remain sovereign and clear of others' energy.

Five Movements of the Breath of Life

We access and regulate the *pranamaya kosha* through the act of breathing, our main source of *prana,* and intentionally through the power of our mind. As this universal life force enters our body it is separated into five "winds" with different movement patterns and functions. These five pranic winds stimulate all bodily processes and govern our health and vitality. Any disruptions or imbalances in the flow of these life force patterns manifest on both the physical and mental planes of our personality. The five major movements of *prana* in the body are as follows:

One: Incoming Energy

Prana vayu, located in the region of the head and chest, moves inward and upward and deals with inspiration, intake, receptivity, and forward momentum and is associated with the heart chakra and brow chakra and the air element. Prana enters through the organs of perception from the food we eat, the air we breathe, the sights we see, the sounds we hear, and through the skin. Imbalances may present as dysfunction in the lungs, heart, brain, and circulatory system.

Two: Outgoing Energy

Apana vayu, located in the pelvic region and lower abdomen, expels downward and outward, deals with elimination movements like perspiration, defecation, and urination. It directs the reproductive processes of ejaculation, menstruation, and childbirth and is associated with the organs below the naval. It is associated with the *muladhara chakra*, the Root Center, and the earth element. Imbalances manifest as dysfunction in organs of elimination and reproduction.

Three: Digestive Energy

Samana vayu, located between the navel and heart, is the balancing energy of the body which deals with multidimensional digestion and assimilation processes and is associated with the *manipura chakra*, the solar plexus, and the element of fire. *Samana vayu* draws energy into the solar plexus center for processing our food, subtle energy, thoughts, and energy from the physical holographic reality. Imbalances can manifest as over or underactive digestive patterns, abdominal discomfort, and gas.

Four: Upward Energy

Udana vayu, located in the throat, has an upward movement and deals with speech, expression, growth, and the upward ascension of prana and kundalini. Associated with the *vishuddha chakra*, *udana vayu* emanates from the throat center in a circular motion around the neck and head, thus assisting with mental clarity and focus. It directs the self-transformation process and the recalibration of willpower to a higher purpose and vision. Imbalances manifest as dysfunction in the throat, neck, and head.

Five: Circulation Energy

Vyana vayu, located in and around the whole body, has an outward from center movement pattern and deals with circulation, expansiveness, and pervasiveness as it directs subtle energy throughout the 72,000 pathways of subtle energy called *nadis* which physicalize as communication networks like the nerves and fascial grid. This movement provides a connection between the senses, nerves, tissues, cells, and the mind creating a feeling of wholeness and containment. This circulatory movement is associated with the *svadhisthana chakra*, the sacral center, and the element of water. Imbalances manifest as feeling unstable, containerless, and clumsy. Overall, the imbalance manifests as systemic dysfunctions of the body

There is an ancient saying that says something like, "If you can extend the length of your breath, you can extend the length of your life." Our quality of breathing, from day to day, determines our quality of living. As we train the breath, we become more radiant and vital. Many spiritual and mystical traditions revere the transformative power of the breath. Life can be thought of as one long breath cycle starting from the first inhalation as a newborn to the last breath of life. Breathing transforms our experience of time. Fast, shallow breathing is parallel to the experience of rush or not enough time. Slow and steady breathing brings us to the present moment where time endlessly unfolds in the eternal NOW.

Hara Line: Bridging Heaven and Earth

You are connected to universal life force and the regenerative consciousness field of Gaia by a pillar of Light that passes through the center of the body, which I call the hara line or pranic tube, or the sushumna nadi when speaking about the physical body. This pranic tube is the axis of the toroidal field of your auric field.

This subtle energy tube tethers us to the subtle planes and the electromagnetic fields of planet Earth. This is our lifeline and our connection to our battery. When we are in the states of love and trust, this pathway is open and clear. When we are in the states of fear and separation consciousness, we are severed from our battery, and we lose life force.

Our hara line, our pranic tube, is the main intake and outtake pathway of our subtle energy body and supplies our chakras with energy from Source and Gaia. When we have a healthy hara line, we feel centered in our being, connected to Source and Gaia, and alive and aligned with our Divine Purpose and the Divine Will of the Universe. We feel energized, alert, and connected to Higher Love.

When our hara line is distorted and blocked, we can feel a myriad of physical, mental, emotional, and spiritual issues. In my opinion, most, if not all, issues stem from hara line distortions and misalignment since the chakras also lay on this major pathway.

Pranic Tube Meditation

Sit or stand so that your spine is erect, and you feel comfortable. Begin to breathe into your hara line and heart until you feel calm and present. Imagine that there is a shining, golden-white star far above your head. This will symbolize your Source, God/Goddess/All That Is.

Invite and imagine that a flowing stream of energy flows down from Source and passes through your crown, all the way through the body, and down into the Earth. Breath this Source Light into your Hara, into your womb, filling it with pure, clear, golden-white energy. Exhale and send the energy down into the Earth. Repeat this breathing pattern a few times and allow this pure Source Energy to sweep away any stagnant or dense energy and release it down into the Earth to be composted. This will not harm the planet. She lovingly takes all our sorrows and struggles and transforms them for us.

Bring your hands onto your heart and feel your own heart's energy. Breathe into it and help it shine. Intend to sense Gaia's heart. Intend to connect to her pulsating rhythm of love. Begin to breathe her love and evolutionary coding up through your hara line into your own heart. Fill your heart with this love and as you exhale, send this love back to Source. Continue a few more times, breathing all this love up into the body and feel Gaia's heart, your heart, and the heart of Creation flowing together and synchronizing.

Bring your hands down to your lap and breathe normally. Sense what has shifted and enjoy your moment. When you are finished, feel blessed to have this connection and open your eyes.

Pranic Tube Tune-Up and Boundaries

Throughout the day, you can clear out your hara line and realign with your Divine Purpose. Simply use conscious breathing, intention, and imagination. As you inhale, bring the energy down from Source into your hara channeling down the Divine Presence, then exhale, grounding the energy into Gaia. Inhale drawing earth energy up from the core of Gaia into your heart. Exhale, send the energy back to Source fully establishing the bridge. Inhale from Gaia and Source, then exhale, radiating light outward, re-establishing your field's boundaries. Make your entire "breathing space" illuminated with compassionate presence. Repeat the pattern until you reach the desired state of stability, peace, and wholeness. In just three breath cycles, you can completely refresh and revitalize your entire energy system and your consciousness and avoid unnecessary suffering.

Nadis

Nadis, Sanskrit for "river channel," are pathways for our subtle energy to move throughout our bioelectric system. The physical manifestation of the nadis include the nerves and fascial grid. Some ancient texts say that there are over 72,000 nadis that weave a matrix of light around and within your body that lead to every cell of your physicality. The three major nadis as called *ida*, *pingala*, and *sushumna*.

Ida and Pingala

Ida and *pingala nadis*, related to the vagus nerves, represent the feminine and masculine polarities of our personality. These two serpent energies weave through our chakra system to create conduits of consciousness that meet in the Brow Center. These two energy pathways play such an important role in health and wellness that the symbol of the *caduceus* has been used by the medical/healing world for a long time. This symbol is depicted as the wand that Hermes or Mercury carries in Greek and Roman mythology.

Ida nadi, the feminine pathway, starts in the root chakra on the left and weaves its way up through the chakras finishing at our left nostril at the brow center. Often associated with the moon, this feminine energy is considered reflective, intuitive, cooling, and nurturing and is described as the mental force, *manas shakti*. This current is active when the left nostril is flowing, and the right hemisphere of the brain is active.

Pingala nadi, the masculine pathway, begins at the root chakra on the right and weaves its way up through the chakras finishing at the right nostril at the brow center. Often associated with solar qualities, this masculine power directs life force energy, *prana shakti*, to energize all essential life processes and is related to heat, logic, assertiveness, and action. This current is active when the right nostril is flowing, and the left-brain hemisphere is activated.

As we breathe in and out through our nose, air carries subtle energy through these two pathways to clear and revitalize the chakra system. As we switch between our consciousness's masculine and feminine qualities, one or the other pathways become dominant. Although without balance and awareness, we can either overstress our energy systems or become lethargic.

The most direct and transformative way I know to balance the masculine and feminine qualities of our consciousness is through the alternate nostril breathing technique, *nadi shodhanam,* and the system of hatha yoga. That being said, all effective healing and personal transformational processes inherently involve the balancing of these polarities.

Sushumna Nadi and Kundalini Shakti

The *sushumna* is the part of our hara line related to our physical body and the seven-chakra system. This tube of light charges and energizes the chakra system. It runs from the base of the spine at the perineum up to the crown of the head. At the base of the *sushumna,* wrapped around the base of the spine, lies the *kundalini shakti,* the ecstatic expression and spiritual potential of your spiritual being.

The *kundalini* energy is said to sit coiled at the base of the spine in *muladhara chakra,* the Root Center. As a soul progresses through incarnations, certain interactions begin to activate this dormant energy and it begins to rise up through *sushumna* balancing the polarities of each chakra as it makes its upward ascension. These two polarities eventually join at the Brow Center to create an experience that some call *Hieros Gamos,* which refers to this alchemical unification of the twin flame polarities within which is the goal of *hatha yoga* practices. Once this has occurred, *kundalini* can make its full ascension to the Crown Center to create the experience called *moksha, nirvana,* salvation, or any of the other names which describe fully realized Godself Consciousness.

Kundalini awakening can be felt like a surge of electrical current from the root of the spine into the higher energy centers of the brow and crown chakras. This can be experienced with body tremors, waves of wisdom and insight, waves of ecstasy, spontaneous mudras and positionings of the body, big emotional shifts, visionary experiences, sensory overload, and more.

Kundalini shakti, the ecstatic, spiritual potential within one's consciousness, begins to rise up the spine and activate each chakra and balance the consciousness at each center on its ascension towards the crown. For most people, *kundalini* rises and then goes back to rest in the Root Center while the practitioner reconciles their consciousness. Progress in one life carries over to the next life. Many "spiritual people" or those on the awakening path have had *kundalini* activation in previous lives and will continue this lifetime working in the chakra that they left off with in the "previous" incarnation. It is said that most of those on the "spiritual path" have at least activated the first three chakras and are beginning to work towards the heart chakra.

As humanity ascends, the awakening of the serpent energies can be quite powerful and intoxicating. As we heal and integrate our consciousness's masculine and feminine qualities, we awaken and stir our creative, sexual-spiritual energies. It is important to learn practices of grounding to work with these energies effectively and safely.

Ascension alchemy practices like Ancient Egyptian sex magic, true tantra, and kundalini and hatha yoga are designed to awaken these energy systems, purify them, and unify our consciousness with the Absolute. While it can be intoxicating and exhilarating to stay in states of kundalini activation, it is also important to ingest foods and participate in activities that nourish and soothe our nervous systems so that we do not "burn out" or overstress them. I recommend seeking out a teacher or a guide who can safely guide you through kundalini awakening if you are feeling unstable through your awakening process.

Chakras: Lenses to See the World

Emerging from *sushumna* channel, we have the blooming of seven main energy vortexes commonly known as the "*chakras.*" The chakra system goes by different names in different traditions. These seals/wheels/lamps/vortices tether our physical body with our subtle body processes. They are toroidal in shape and always in states of movement and evolution. They contain life force energy as well as mental energy. Like individual minds, each contains our programmed beliefs about the seven major areas of our life, such as community and physical life, self-identity and relationships, willpower, compassion, communication, vision, and universality. Besides the seven main chakras, there are many sub-chakras and micro-chakras throughout the body with some existing outside of the body. However, these seven are the most important when cultivating consciousness liberation and holistic wellness.

Each of the seven main chakras relates to certain glands in the endocrine system, nerve plexi, and particular organs and bodily systems. As energy information passes through the aura, it is processed through the chakra system and creates emotional/mental/physical experiences based on our beliefs and previous experiences with similar dynamics. This energy ripples out across the subtle energy pathways (nadis/meridians) into the nervous system and endocrine system to create sensations, bodily functions, and events.

Chakra Locations

Here are the locations of the seven main chakras, the two minor chakras, and the three newly emerging ascension chakras:
- **Soul Star Center:** Felt 6-12 inches above the head
- **Crown Center:** Crown of the head
- **Brow Center:** Between the forehead and occiput
- **Zeal Center:** Emanating from the medulla oblongata, attachment point of the spine to the skull
- **Throat Center:** Center of the throat
- **Heart Center:** Felt between and behind the manubrium and xiphoid process of the sternum
- **Solar Plexus Center:** Just below the diaphragm
- **Sacral Center:** Low abdomen behind the naval
- **Root Center:** Base of the spine at the pelvic floor
- **Earth Star Center:** Below the feet when standing, below the pelvis when seated
- **Palm Chakras:** Center of the palms
- **Foot Chakras:** Soles of the feet

Chakra Filaments: How We Feel Our Environment

Chakras radiate filaments of light, just like the rays and filaments of the sun. The number of filaments on a chakra relates to the frequency of the chakra. The higher the frequency, the higher the number of petals opening from the electromagnetic flower.

These filaments reach out to interact with a specific layer of our auric field. Picture a plasma ball from science class with the violet plasma whipping across the inside of the glass globe. Each filament reaches through its environment to absorb the energy information in the world around us while simultaneously broadcasting our essence into the field. The chakras respond to our attention. As we focus our energy on an object, they begin to drink in the energy of the object of our attention.

Attachments and Cords

When we develop an attachment to an object, our energy forms a habit of focusing on the object of our attention. Unhealthy relationships are a result of unhealthy beliefs and a habit of attaching our energy to the object. They are habits of where we direct our life force. Cords develop between people that relate in unhealthy ways, thus creating codependent patterns.

To reconcile this once you become aware of an unhealthy relationship, practice the Hara Line Aura Meditation and return to sovereign alignment with the Source Within You. To create permanent change, you can work on identifying and shifting your belief systems that caused the unhealthy patterns, or they will return later until you fully see and heal this part of your subconscious.

Distortion in Our Subtle Bodies

Even before we are born, we begin to absorb the mental patterning of the world beyond our mother's womb. Some people experience trauma within the womb and carry it throughout their life. Additionally, our DNA is filled with energy information from the lifetimes of those who came before us who passed down the genetic coding through our lineages. As mentioned before, life experiences also reactivate stored information in our causal body that brings forth patterns created in past lives.

Traumatic life experiences, memories, and energies often get trapped in all layers of the bodymind complex. Slowly over time, they release so that we do not feel the full brunt of the psychophysical trauma at the moment of the event. When energy is not reconciled, the bodymind tries to release the energy in some way. This can look like crying, sighing, shaking, screaming, sleeping, illness, dreams, and so on. If we practice meditation and self-healing, we can speed up our recovery process significantly.

If we suppress or ignore our emotions and trapped energy, the negative effects begin to show up in our physical bodies. Over time patterns begin to crystallize and become more physical as the bodymind tries to eliminate the distorted energy information. From the most subtle inflammation to the most aggressive cancer, it all has its roots in the subtle energy system. We can use our conscious awareness to reconcile traumatic injuries in our bodies and return to wholeness and vitality.

The *chakras* are constantly broadcasting our internal world and magnetizing events to them that reflect the stored subconscious beliefs. The distortions and trauma stored within our subconscious show up in our life as manifestations of similar circumstances that trigger the trauma patterning. This "clashing" brings our unconscious patterns to the surface so that we can exhaust and potentially integrate the energy information from the past experience and grow in consciousness maturity. From this perspective, we can understand how we create our reality and how everything truly begins within our very own consciousness. As within, so without.

With conscious awareness and subtle energy healing techniques, you can unpack the information stored within the emotions, thought patterns, and physical body events and reconcile the energy. This naturally brings a deeper understanding, and wisdom is revealed through the healing process. This frees up the pathways so that energy can flow freely, and we experience a more joyful, conscious life.

Illness and disease are the body's intelligence giving us a massive wake-up call to tune into our inner being and create a rich, inner life that is luminous and vital. As we tune into subtle energy, we unlock the mysteries of the bodymind's intelligence and begin to accelerate in consciousness growth and authentic empowerment.

Pranayama: Entering the Dimension of Prana

Breathing is one of the main ways that we regulate the movement of the life force in the body. Each inhalation brings in fresh, new life force energy to be used by the body's cells and systems. Each exhalation expels old stagnant energy that is no longer needed by the body. One of the secrets to living a long and vibrant life is the power of conscious breathing.

Breath cycles are made of four stages. *Puraka*, a deep, rich inhalation, focuses the mind and energizes the cells and systems of the body. Inner breath retention, *antar kumbhaka*, equally distributes, calms, and clarifies prana. Conscious exhalation, *rechaka*, releases toxins and calms the bodymind. External breath retention, *bahya kumbhaka*, moves *prana* up the spine to the brain and creates a sense of non-attachment, peace, and inner silence. Women who are pregnant and people with high blood pressure, lung, heart, eye, or ear problems should not hold either phase of breath retention. Instead, they should focus only on the inhalation and exhalations.

Below is a descriptive list of breathing practices, called *pranayama* by the ancient yogis, to get you started with the basics. When you first begin practicing *pranayama*, start with learning to equalize the duration of the inhalation and exhalations in a 1:1 ratio (using a count of four or five seconds) with a slight pause in between inhalation and exhalation. Then increase exhalation duration by doubling the number in a 1:2 ratio. Once this is mastered, add in inhalation breath retention for a ratio of 1:2:2. For more advanced practices, I recommend checking out the *Hatha Yoga Pradipika*.

As you do these practices, keep an easy mind and relaxed body while sitting in a tall, meditative posture. If at any point you feel frustration or tension, stop the practice, return to neutral, and start again when you are ready.

Another practice that I highly recommend is the use of a *neti* pot which looks somewhat like a tea pot and is used for a sinus washing process that clears obstructions out of the nasal passageway. This practice called *jala neti* will increase the body's absorption of prana during breathing and help to awaken subtle consciousness in the brow center.

Three-Part Breathing or Yogic Breathing (Dirga Pranayam)

This breathing style incorporates the full range of breathing capacity utilizing abdominal, thoracic, and clavicular breathing awareness. This practice oxygenates and nourishes the whole body and is great for reducing anxiety and stress.

First, exhale completely until you feel the lower abdomen contract and the pelvic floor lift. Softly release the lower abdomen and allow it to expand with your inhale. After the abdomen expands, allow the chest to expand, feel the energy of the inhale rise up through your spine and into the crown of your head. Softly exhale and reverse the process and allow the air and energy to drain down from the head, softening the chest, exhaling completely until the lower abdomen contracts and the pelvic floor lifts. Repeat, softly extending each segment of the cycle of breath. As you do this, you can imagine that you are surrounded by brilliant, clear, white light. With each breath, you can breathe this fresh light into all the cells of the body.

Samma Vritti: Equal Flow Box Breath

This breathing practice is called "box breath" as the patterning can be thought of as the equal dimensions of a square with inhalation, breath retention after inhalation, exhalation, and breath retention after exhalation. Start simply with a count of four during each stage. Then you can increase the number as you develop control and calmness of the bodymind within each stage. This can be done with regular yogic breathing as well as in alternate nostril breathing.

Kapalbhati: Skull-Cleansing Breath

This breathing practice gets its name because of its revitalizing and healing properties. *Kapalbhati* clears the mind, burns away stagnant energy, clears the respiratory system, and brightens the face and higher chakras. In this practice, inhalations are relaxed, and deep and rapid force is applied to the exhale.

Pregnant or menstruating women should not do this practice nor should people with spinal injuries. If you have high blood pressure, stomach ulcers, or any other health issues, be gentle (one pump per second) until you see how the body works with the practice.

Using the three-part breathing, inhale fully and allow the belly and chest to fill with air. On the exhale, contract the abdomen strongly back towards the spine, feeling a strong pulse of air exit the nose. Softly relax the abdomen and allow the lungs to fill with air. Repeat this pattern, slowly increasing the cycles' speed, creating a rapid breathing pattern that is also relaxed in mind and emotions.

Repeat for around twenty to thirty rounds. On the last exhale, gently push out all the excess air until you feel the pelvic floor and abdomen contract. Drop the chin towards the chest and gently lift the heart towards the chin to make an energetic lock. Hold for a few moments, then release the head and soften the throat, abdomen, and pelvic floor. Find a neutral position of the spine and return to normal conscious breathing and observe your internal experience. If it feels right, you can add consecutive rounds of practice.

Bhastrika: Bellows Breath

Bellows Breath energizes the mind and body, tones the abdominal muscles, and builds the digestive fire. This is a great practice to do if you are feeling tired, confused, or sluggish. It focuses on equal force of inhales and exhales. The practice is often done with arm movement to help with the expansion and contraction of the lungs.

Sit comfortably and find your natural, three-part breathing. After a complete exhale, bring your arms up above your head, spreading the fingers wide as you reach for the sky, and inhale deeply with gentle force. Exhale by strongly contracting the abdomen towards the spine while simultaneously closing the fingers into fists and pulling the elbow down towards the ribs, contracting the muscles of your arms and abdomen fully as you exhale. Inhale deeply to raise the arms back up above the head and repeat the cycle for twenty to thirty rounds. After you exhale, bring the arms down, rest the hands on the legs or ground, and observe your inner experience. If desired, you can repeat the practice.

Bhramari Breath: Bee Breath

Bhramari Breath uses breath and toning of the vocal cords to send vibrations through the throat and skull. The long exhalations assist the autonomic nervous system by inducing a relaxation response through the lengthened exhales. This practice is excellent for anyone who needs to calm the mind and focus their intention.

Sit comfortably in your meditation posture and do several rounds of full yogic breathing. Raise both hands in front of the face with your elbows pointing outwards, in line with the shoulders, with the palms facing you. Close your eyes, gently press the index fingers to the inner corners of the eyes, place the middle fingers on either side of the nose, the ring fingers above the lips, and the little fingers below the mouth. Use the thumbs to gently close the ears.

Another option is to take your hands and rub them together, activating them with light and energy. Bring the hands up to each side of the head, blocking the ears by pressing lightly on the tragus of each ear to close the ear canal. Take the other fingers and lightly touch the brow with the pads of the fingers. Fingers should be spread across the forehead and hairline.

Once your hand position is set you can begin the "bee's breath." At the top of the inhale, begin to make a humming sound with the lips closed. Draw out the sound and play with the pitch of the tones. Feel the vibrations moving throughout your nostrils, sinuses, throat, and brain. Imagine that your hands' vibrations and energy pulsations are breaking apart unhealthy thought patterns and upgrading the neural pathways. Fill the skull and throat with vibrations. Do this for about six rounds. Then drop the mudra and sound and feel the subtle shifts happening along the pathways of energy.

Nadi Shodhanam: Alternate Nostril Breathing

Alternate nostril breathing balances the right and left hemispheres of the brain and the masculine and feminine principles of consciousness, creating a state of calm focus. This practice is especially useful when you feel anxiety or stress. It is a wonderful practice to do before you start anything that needs your full attention and awareness. There are a variety of methods to do alternate nostril breathing. Here is a basic practice:

Take the index and middle fingers of the right hand and lightly touch the center of the brow. You will be using the inside of the ring finger and the pad of the thumb to block and alternate the passage of air through the nostrils. The other hand can be resting on your lap, in jnana mudra, resting on your heart, or in any other comfortable position.

Using the thumb, gently press against the outside of the nose to close the right nostril and exhale completely through the left nostril, gently contracting the lower abdomen and pelvic floor at the bottom of the exhale. Then breathe in through the left nostril as you release the abdominal contraction. Feel the air and energy circulating in the center of the brow under the fingertips. Gently pause at the top without adding tension to the face or upper torso.

Switch nostrils, block the left nostril with the inside of the ring finger, release the thumb off the right nostril, and exhale through the right nostril until you feel the abdomen and pelvic floor contract. Pause for a moment. Then breathe in through the right nostril feeling the air circulate at the brow. Pause again.

Close the right nostril, open the left nostril, and exhale through the left until you feel the abdominal and pelvic floor contractions.

Repeat for at least two to three minutes or longer. Meditate on smoothing out and evening each segment of the breath. A suggestion of ratio would be to start first with a 1:1 ratio, building up to 1:2.

Combined Practice Suggestion:

- 3 rounds kapalbhati (30-50 pulses per round)
- 2 rounds of Bhastrika (30-50 pulses per round)
- 3 complete breaths (natural breathing)
- 3 rounds of nadi shodhanam (2-3 minutes per round)
- 2-3 minutes of bhramari
- Breath awareness
- Meditation

For a shorter practice, you can skip the *bhastrika* breath and keep the cleansing benefits of *kapalbhati*.

Circular Breathing

This breathing practice goes by many names, some of which are trademarked. This type of breathwork involves deep, continuous breathing cycles that highly oxygenate the body and reduce carbon dioxide. This circular breathing pattern is known to help reduce depression, process and integrate trauma, eliminate fears and phobias, and much more. It is known to induce altered states of consciousness and awaken unconscious memory for processing and integration. Many people report having psychedelic-like experiences. It is not recommended to do this practice if you have cardiac or respiratory health issues. Go gentle at first and see how you respond, then you can decide whether to increase or reduce the intensity or duration of the practice. It is recommended to do these practices with a trained facilitator who can guide you through emotional experiences, involuntary muscle spasms, or other powerful experiences. If you are doing this practice alone, go gently and feel it out.

1. Lay down on a flat and comfortable surface. You may wish to cover yourself with a blanket. Keep the head flat on the ground, no pillow, so that the spine stays long and even.
2. Start with a progressive relaxation body scan.
3. Begin the circular breathing pattern with deep inhalations and deep exhalations, no pausing in between. Try to make it seamless.
4. Be careful not to push or strain the body. Back off the edge a bit.
5. Pick up the speed. Do it a little faster than normal but not so fast that the body tenses.
6. It is perfectly normal and common for the face muscles or the hands or feet to contract. Keep breathing through it, nice and gently.
7. If fear or other powerful emotions arise, breathe through them. You can back off the intensity a bit if you wish.
8. Do the practice for about 10-20 minutes. Then relax completely and feel the effects for another 10 minutes or so.

The Microcosmic Orbit

The microcosmic orbit circulates life force throughout the entire system of the body. Sit mindfully and quiet the mind by bringing your awareness to your breath. Bring the tongue to touch the back of the teeth and roof of the mouth to close the "heavenly gate" and gently lift the pelvic floor to close the "earthly gate." This creates an energetic loop that connects the front and back of the body. Breathe mindfully into the pelvis and imagine that the pelvic bowl is filling with white light. As you inhale, sweep the white light towards your sacrum and up your spine, cresting at the top of the head. As you exhale, sweep the white light down the front of your face and body and back to your pelvis. Continue circulating your awareness, breath, and the white light through this orbit until you feel clear, clean, and balanced in your energy. When you are finished, simply return to regular conscious breathing, and observe your Inner Being's sensations.

Pranic Body Summary

We are a bridge between the higher consciousness realms and Earth, existing in an ever-changing matrix of subtle energy. We access this connection through our hara line and personal energy field. As energy information passes through our energy field, it is dispersed to energy vortexes called chakras, transforming the data through our belief center programming, creating emotions. Emotions pulse out a charge of energy that fractals out along the nadis/meridians to create physical body processes and our perception of ourselves and the world around us. We can use the power of our breathing and breath awareness to reconcile our consciousness and return all systems to health and balance. As we raise our vibration and awareness, we move beyond the need for illness and disease as a teacher of karma and move into the perfection of our Divine Blueprint as conscious embodiments of the Breath of Life.

TWO

Wheels of Light

*"Behold, I stand at the door and knock: if any person hears my voice
and opens the door, I will come into their being and will sup with them,
and they with me."* Revelation 3:20

To sup is to drink liquid or liquid food. Yeshua ben Joseph often talked about water and the quenching of thirst. To truly quench your soul's thirst, one needs to discover what desire is at the core of thirst. What is at the core of hunger? What truly nourishes and satiates hunger? What truly quenches thirst?

True nourishment comes from union with the Divine. We, as humanity, have had the Light of Source knock on our own Crown Chakra. It is up to us to acknowledge and welcome the Higher Consciousness Reality into our being, to bring Heaven to Earth through our bodies. We can invite the "dove" of the Holy Spirit to descend through our Crown Chakra and begin to transform us from within.

We, as a species, are being invited to step out of mundane, biological evolution and cycles of karmic suffering into a higher spiritual evolution called Ascension. We are being invited to lay down our weapons of ignorance and receive the Light of Truth in our very hands, hearts, and minds.

Let us accept the Higher Realms and the truth of the pathway of Ascension and welcome the Higher Light into our being. Let us eat and be satiated. Let us drink from the eternal waters of Higher Wisdom and Compassion and let the depths of our thirst be quenched. The door is open and available for all souls to release their attachment to the conditioning of the world and open to the pure Light and Love of our Source.

To receive our Divine Inheritance, it is essential that we learn to see beyond the illusion of duality-based polarized mindsets and unite our awareness with our True Nature and the Divine Presence. This process involves activating our lightbody and purifying the physical, etheric, and mental bodies of any contamination and distortions. As we "wash our robes," we begin to connect with deeper spiritual truth and liberate ourselves from our own karmic creations and their repercussions. As we do this, we naturally become agents of cosmic spiritual transformation through every atom of our being.

Chakra Yoga is the process of recalibrating our subtle energy body and fortifying our energy centers through spiritual practice. Each chakra is a lens of perception that can be cleansed and cleared of distortions that keep us in cycles of karmic entanglement and suffering. To step off the Wheel of Karma, *samsara*, it is essential that we liberate each chakra and its associated mental patterning from the conditionings of the world and update each of these processing centers with Higher Wisdom and Truth. This is how we can be "in the world but not of it." We can train our mind to see beyond the 3D duality-based matrix into a higher perspective of Unity and Divinity.

The ancient spiritual teachings of *Advaita Vedanta* give four qualifications (*sadhana chatustaya*) for an aspirant who wishes to unify their consciousness with the Divine and achieve full self-realization. If you are reading this book, you likely have some level of all of these. Our work is to continue to continue to develop these skills:

Viveka — Discrimination: Discrimination is the quality of mind to discern between what is transient and what is constant in past, present, and future (Brahman/Absolute Reality). This ability to distinguish what is real versus what is an illusion, what is permanent, and what is impermanent withdraws one's mind from the snares of *samsara*, the cycles of suffering, so that one can focus their mind on Higher Truth and their True Nature.

Vairagya — Dispassion or Non-Attachment: Dispassion is the quality of having an absence of desire for enjoying the fruits of one's labor. Since true fulfillment comes from alignment with our True Self, the aspirant becomes increasingly aware of when they believe their source of fulfillment is from outside of themself. Spiritual growth and the attainment of true, lasting happiness is truly an inside job.

Shadsampathi — Six-Fold Inner Wealth: A spiritual aspirant needs the discipline to focus their efforts to achieve all the fruits of ascension. As we learn to *master the mind (sama)* and *master the senses (dama)* by focusing them on our path of awakening, we repattern our mind to *automatically meditate on the Divine Presence (uparati)*. Spiritual growth is not linear; it has ups and downs, so we need to cultivate *endurance and perseverance towards our goal of awakening (titiksha)*. We do this through *faith in the sacred texts and the teachings of the enlightened masters* which guide us on the path of awakening to the Divine *(shraddha)*. All these qualities merge so that we can have a *single-pointed mind focused on the Divine (samadhana)*.

Mumukshatavam — Desire for Moksha or Liberation: This is the desire above all desires. It is born from the clear knowing that "the world" is illusion and that true happiness and fulfillment is an inside job. The desire for true and lasting liberation fuels the process of awakening and secures your footing on the dharmic path. Whatever you do in your moment-to-moment living, use it for the purpose of unifying with the God-force within you. Use every activity of your life as a spiritual practice for unification with your True Self.

In summary, as we grow in the capacity to discriminate between what is permanent and what is impermanent, we learn to detach from the ways of the world to focus our life on the Divine. As we learn to master our mind and senses, our focus on the Divine becomes automatic. Through perseverance and faith in the sacred teachings, we develop cohesive focus and deliberate action to fulfill our desire of true liberation from cycles of suffering and union with the true source of our happiness and wholeness.

Yeshua ben Joseph, Jesus the Christ, exemplified the discipline needed to walk the dharmic path fully. To accomplish his soul's mission, he had to completely clear his mind of all distortion so that he could maintain a single-minded focus on the Divine. No matter how much pain was inflicted, no matter what was promised to him by "the world," he followed his dharmic path all the way through.

A christ-conscious being is an ambassador of the radiant Wisdom and Knowledge of the Divine in full Service to the Greater Good of All. Whether one calls it Krishnahood, Buddhahood, or Christhood does not matter. The path is still the same. Once we no longer need anything from the world to bring us happiness, we stand as fully illumined beings in Service to All!

This next section of *The Illumination Codex* material is a deep dive discourse into the seven-chakra system commonly known through the practices of Hatha Yoga. I also include additional chakras that are beginning to activate as we shift into the recalibrated, restructured, and updated Fourth Density Adamic Form.

Throughout my years of seeking, I have studied the subtle body through a variety of lenses. I have been most impacted by the literary work of Dr. Synthia Andrews, ND and the video transmissions of Neeta Singal. These two subtle body visionaries have impressive bodies of work. Be sure to check them out!

THREE

Root Chakra: Grounded in Being

The Root Chakra is located at the base of the spine and is associated with the color red. It has a horizontal spin with the vortex opening down towards the legs and up towards the crown. This chakra connects us to the physical world, to our body, food, basic resources, family, and community. It is our connection to our primal instincts and animal nature. It helps us create structure and plans and helps us ground into and expand time while connecting us to the foundations of the physical world, physical body, and the Earth element.

When our Root Chakra is balanced, we feel secure in our environment. We feel stable in our life because we easily tend to the basic structures and systems that support a healthy flow. We feel supported in our life process and easily create a wide network of community bonds with varying degrees of depth. We feel a sense of security in our being and find solitude to be healing and rejuvenating. When our Root Chakra is open and flowing, we feel grounded and supported, and we rest in knowing that all our basic needs are met. This creates a feeling of safety, and we can face any challenges that come our way.

The Root Center connects us with the Earth. While we incarnate on the Earth, we are lovingly and unconditionally supported by Gaia, the soul of the Earth, the Mother of Life on this planet. She does not give for greed, only for need, and provides us with all necessities to keep us healthy and strong.

For example, when walking in the wilderness we may feel inspired to pick some berries from the bushes to eat. As we approach the bush, we can tune into our intention to harvest and tune into Mother Earth and the bush. If we listen closely, we can sense through our inner being if harvesting is appropriate. If we get a sense that it is permitted, we may begin harvesting. At a certain point, we may get an inner impulse that we have harvested enough from that area. We have a choice to give in to our own desires or to honor the communication from the Earth and the bush. We can be grateful for what we have been given and carry on along our path trusting that Mother Nature will continue to provide, or we can succumb to lack-consciousness and steal more from her without her consent. Mother is quite forgiving, and you could take more but it will have an immediate energetic effect. Now multiply that same action of greed across the whole human species and we see why we are in the predicament we are in now with the imbalance and environmental damage rampant across the Earth. If we would have been taught this basic skill of communication with our Earth mother as children, our civilization would be much different. The Indigenous peoples have much to share about living in balance with our Earth Mother.

We will never be without as long as we are open to this connection with the Earth Mother. Like any loving mother, she gives all that she can to support her children so that they can be happy and free. We can lay upon her like a baby lays upon its mother and receive supportive energy. We can explore the world with a sense of safety knowing that Mother is nearby. We can confide in her and release all the density of our soul into the loving arms of our Earth Mother. She is open to receiving all the negativity that we hold onto and happily transmutes it for us.

Imagine that the body is a tree with a wide root system that runs deep into the Earth. You can receive all of the nutrients you need to grow towards the sky and Father/Mother/God. Those connected with the Love of Mother Gaia are like a system of trees, a community that other beings can take refuge in and borrow strength from.

Root Chakra Imbalance

When our root chakra is imbalanced, we are cut off from our connection to the Earth, and survival and lack-consciousness are activated. This can manifest as fears related to resources, time, community bonds, and so on. Overall, a sense of lack creeps in, and we feel isolated, singular, and cut off from the abundance of the world. We may perceive that there just does not seem to be enough to go around. The world seems unsafe, and we begin to seek power outside of ourselves by controlling the external world to survive. Fear, anxiety, and loneliness are symptoms of an imbalanced root chakra.

When the root chakra is overactive, we may find ourselves overcompensating as if we have not done enough or are somehow missing the mark. We may feel struggle as we are cut off from a co-creative relationship with physical reality and feel that everything rests upon our shoulders. We may overemphasize our needs out of fear that we were not heard or understood or that we might miss out on what we desire. Because of this, we may collect things and hoard things because we have a deep-seated fear that there may not be any in the future. We envision a future of lack because we are creating from the belief that there is not enough and that we are not safe.

We may become rigid and over-rooted, making it hard for us to grow and evolve because we are trying so hard to control our external reality to feel safe. We may try to force others to be like us because we do not trust beyond what we know. This fear can keep us stuck in unhealthy situations and relationships because we fear the unknown. We could become like an obedient dog and be loyal no matter how unfulfilling our relationships, jobs, or environments are. If we feel that life is out of control, we could develop unhealthy relationships with food and use food to control our emotions.

If our root chakra is underactive, we may feel unrooted in our life, floating around and unable to commit to anything. We can change jobs and relationships at the first sign of conflict. We become like a little mouse and scurry away, unable to face our fears and challenges. When fear is activated, all the blood leaves our torso and rushes to our legs and arms so that we can fight or flee. Sometimes the fear is so strong that we are frozen in one place, unable to move in any direction emotionally or physically.

The physical manifestation of root chakra imbalances could manifest in the feet, legs, and bones. One may develop knee issues because they are subconsciously afraid to move on their path. One may develop foot issues because they have not fully committed to their dharma and path of growth through incarnating. One may develop excess tension in the body because they are in constant stress and fear. Nervous system issues may develop because of habitual states of nervousness, anxiety, and agitation. These are just a few examples of how Root Center imbalances manifest in the physical body.

What Blocks the Root Chakra?

False Evidence Appearing Real

Fear arises when we feel threatened, overpowered, and undermined. Fear happens when taking information from our past and projecting it into our future. We take limited information and create a story from it. Fear can arise because of an external circumstance like a dangerous situation. It can also originate from subtle subconscious thoughts that mostly operate in the background of our mind unnoticed. Fear is insidious. It eats away at our freedom and keeps us from feeling free. It blocks us from having a higher perspective and seeing the bigger picture.

Many fears originate from unresolved trauma in this lifetime. Fear can also be from other lifetimes, where we experienced past trauma. For instance, someone may have died in a car accident when crossing a bridge and flew out into the water and drowned. Subconsciously, when that person drives across a bridge or near water in this lifetime, fear may begin to creep in and create havoc in their emotions for a seemingly unknown reason. This is the power of the samskaras, the reactive momenta from the past, over our bodymind's expression.

The Root Center and Crown Center work in a symbiotic relationship. When we are afraid, we instantly close our root and crown chakras. We become identified with our "separate self" and feel disconnected from the world. We cut ourselves off from the stability and safety given to us through a clear connection to the Earth field and from the limitlessness of the Universe.

Fear is an invitation to grow in alignment and trust. Even in the most chaotic and dangerous situations, we can still maintain clear trust and presence.

This type of clarity and groundedness can be seen with medical staff who work in the emergency room in hospitals. Fear or anxiety may arise in them, but their job is to ignore the projections of people in pain and focus on making clear and calculated choices to keep their patients alive.

Parents/Caregivers, Family of Origin

Our family of origin sets up the foundation of our beliefs. This includes the root chakra qualities of stability, structure, support, and solitude. This is where we learn how to be a community and how we relate to the world around us. Much of our wounding in this life comes from our childhood and our relationship with our parents and family. These relationships are continuing to play out in our extended community and in our adult relationships. When we complete the emotional healing from our childhood wounding, we can have flourishing relationships with our community and a healthy relationship with life.

The Deification of Parents, Familial Domestication

When we are born, our parents provide us with our initial education about life. From our human perspective, we believe that they are our source of food, resources, shelter, and love. They become the god and goddess of our universe. We deify them and see them as all-knowing and all-powerful beings. They give us a name and begin to transfer to us their knowledge about the world. They begin to transfer their language and definitions to us and teach us their values and perspectives. They tell us who we are and who we are not. They tell us what we are capable of and what we are not capable of. Since we are so small and they hold so much power, we believe them and adopt their laws and beliefs as our own.

Parents need to teach a child how to be in the world to grow up and be happy and successful. Parents can only teach what they have learned from life and their parents. To train young children to be like them, parents establish a system of reward and punishment. When we are a good boy or girl, we get human love and resources. When we do not please them, they can withhold love or resources from us. Since we are dependent on them, we begin to adapt our behavior to please them. This way, we receive love from them and get what we want from them. At a certain point, we learn their system well enough to no longer need them to reward or punish us because we do it for ourselves.

Later in our development, we often begin to question our parents' knowledge and authority as we start to see the flaws in their systems. Sometimes parents encourage their children to go beyond what they have learned, but this is often met with resistance, which can lead to a battle between the child and their parents.

If we experienced or witnessed violence or abuse, we will have fears related to this. If our homes had yelling or fighting, we learned that the world is not safe, people are dangerous, and we can get hurt. We may have learned that we need to watch out because people are violent, the world is a violent place, and we cannot trust people. Because we hold these emotions and energies from our trauma, we attract the same situations into our life so that we can learn deeper truth and return to wholeness.

To fully heal the root chakra, we need to make peace with our parents and our siblings. This does not mean that our parents need to change, but we can evolve and do the internal work necessary to heal our wounds from childhood so that we feel safe and secure in our life. This does not mean that we have to condone the actions of our abusers, but we can acknowledge that they behaved in the way they did because they were suffering. Compassion and forgiveness are the way out of the karmic bonds created through abuse.

Ancestral Lineage Imprinting

Many of our family beliefs and emotional patterns started long ago in our family histories. We are a collection of our maternal and paternal lines of knowledge and experience. What was not healed and integrated from previous generations is passed along to the next generations. This information is stored in the DNA of our bodies as micro-packets of information and mental fields. While some of the emotional, mental, and biological patterns skip generations, certain patterns reactivate in later generations. This is seen in hereditary diseases, where the echoes of ancestral trauma continue to wreak havoc on the biology, mental attitudes, and emotional patterns of modern generations. Epigenetics studies the ability to alter the DNA to create harmonic gene expression. We can abandon the fate of heredity and choose health and vitality by evolving beyond our ancestors' inherited mental and emotional patterns. Here are some questions you can use as part of your own ancestral wound healing process:

- How attached are you to your family identity?
- What role do you have in your family? Was it self-proclaimed or projected onto you?
- How did you respond to your parents' authority as a child? How did you cope?
- Were there instances or patterns of neglect? Physical abuse? Sexual abuse? Mental abuse? Emotional abuse?
- Have you forgiven your parents for what they did in states of ignorance?
- Are you able to fully send love to your parents and siblings?

- What mental attitudes have you adopted from your family?
- How has your parents' relationship with one another been reflected in your own intimate relationships?
- What was your childhood relationship with your Mother? With your Father? How do those dynamics play out in your adult relationships?
- Where do you still give power away to your parents? What causes you to become critical or return to the "child seat?"
- Tracing back through your family lineages, where did the traumas begin? What hereditary illnesses sprang from those traumas?

Money

Parents pass along their beliefs about money and resources such as "You have to work hard to make money." or "There is never enough to go around." We may have distortions in the root chakra if one of our parents lost their jobs or if money was a concern and our parents talked about it or fought about it in front of us. Since we are so devoted to our parents and see them as all-knowing beings (deifying), we believe them and take on their beliefs consciously and subconsciously.

Whatever work we do in the world, let it be done as an act of devotion by bringing our full spirit into the work and acting from a place of selfless service (karma yoga). If we are doing our work primarily for money or external reasons, we quickly drain the joy out of our experience since money and success are temporarily satisfying. This does not mean we should not receive compensation for our efforts but that we should instead find the richness and security that lives within, and then everything else is a bonus.

If we look back over our lifetime, we will see that we always had the basic resources to get us by. We were always able to find what we needed eventually. We may have had to ask a friend or borrow something from someone, but we were always provided for in the end. Solutions are always available. If we can release beliefs around lack and trust that all is being provided for us, we open the gates for more abundance to flow in.

- What are your beliefs around money? Positive and negative?
- What are your parents' beliefs about money, finances, and work?

- How did you hear your parents talking about finances and wealth?
- Where do you think money comes from? How does that relate to the laws of the universe?
- Do you have any fears about your basic needs being met or the future of your finances and stability?

Community

The way we experience our community and relationships is a collection of many facets, including the initial patterns we learned from our family of origin, cultural attitudes, and subconscious patterning from other lifetimes. We see these subconscious patterns out picturing in our relationships. We can use our community members as divine mirrors to reflect where we are in our current state of consciousness development.

We do not need to stay in any toxic relationship any longer. Once we become aware of the subconscious fears that keep us in isolation and loneliness patterns, we can release those patterns and form a new path for ourselves. Find a community of people that love and accept you. There is much love out there for you. Be brave and build bridges wherever you go. Say hello to strangers and open the door for people. Connect with your Inner Light and smile at people with your whole being as you pass. Look into the clerk's eyes at the store with radiant love and allow yourself to be seen. Build a network of connection and love.

- Do you feel safe in your home? In your community? Workplace? Nation?
- What are your general beliefs about people?
- How do your beliefs affect how you walk in the world?
- Do you feel like you belong? Do you think others do not belong?
- Do you find yourself trusting others?

Fear of Instability

If we experience unstable conditions in this life or other lifetimes, we can hold that fear of instability in our energy signature. When we project our fears into the future, we create them.

We are not helpless victims, enslaved by the patterns of our past. We are powerful, Divine Creators, and we are always being provided with what we need to sustain and raise our quality of life. The tighter we grip life and attempt to control it from a state of fear, the more things go awry. Trust that you are being provided with everything that you need and envision a future of opulence and ease.

- Do you have fears about not having enough to make ends meet?
- Do you have a positive or fearful perspective of the future?
- How do you feel your life is going to progress?
- Do you find yourself saving up for when things go bad?
- Are you often waiting for the "other shoe to drop?"
- Do you feel guided by the Divine? Supported by the Earth?

Physical and Mental Attachments

Attachments are a way for us to distract ourselves from our true source of pleasure and life force. Our alignment is what truly feeds us and brings us joy. It may seem like our body, our car, our lover, or our XYZ brings us joy and pleasure. The truth is it always comes from our experience of allowing our alignment with the Source Within Us and our ability to trust in the Universe.

Where does your safety come from? Where does abundance come from? Where does your joy come from? Do you fear losing XYZ and the suffering that it would bring?

Fear of Change and Impermanence

Everything is constantly changing and evolving. When we fear change, we try to control our environment's external circumstances, and we keep ourselves from growing and evolving. We need to become comfortable with the unknown and trust that we are being supported through the process. Many stay in cycles of suffering and limited perception because they fear the Mystery. They go with what they know because the Void of the Unknown scares them. We can make peace with the Void and allow ourselves to navigate the uncharted waters of our consciousness.

- Where do you resist change? What do you cling to?
- Do you trust in your ability to navigate uncharted waters and new experiences?

- Do you actively seek paradigm shifts and growth?

Struggle

The belief that we need to struggle to succeed generates patterns of struggle in our lives. The struggle is resistance, and when we are experiencing resistance to what is currently manifested, we cut ourselves off from the loving guidance and intelligence of our inner Source.

When we believe that life is hard or that life or God is against us, we keep ourselves from being able to access the part of our being that is connected to divine guidance, and we create from a sense of lack. Be solution-oriented, forgiving, easy, and gentle. Be optimistic, open, patient, and present. Do not take life so seriously. Nothing is so serious. When we are met with challenges, we can take a deep breath and open ourselves to receive the solution.

- Do you feel working hard makes you more valuable?
- Do you find yourself constantly busy?
- Do you have a "no pain, no gain" attitude?

Laziness and Sloth: Physical Effort, Training the Body

The root chakra also governs our beliefs about the use of our body and how we show up physically in our lives. The body enjoys being strengthened, toned, and developed. The more we use our body, the more grounded and stable we feel in our body. The body is like a horse that you need to train. Make it sweat; feed it healthy foods; make it strong; test its abilities.

The more we give in to feelings of laziness and sluggishness, the weaker we feel, and we begin to wither away. If we procrastinate and delay doing what our life is asking us to do, our body takes a toll. If we have an aversion to physical effort, we can tune into what beliefs create the resistance. Was it something from our past? Are we afraid of being tired? Why are we unmotivated? When we are willing to show up and do the work, we grow in confidence and stamina.

At the same time, if we are not listening to our body's requests, we can become overworked and drained. This is usually happening because we are working from a place of fear.

Quiet your mind and tune into your impulses. What is driving you? What are you running from? The work is never done, and the list will never be completed. Take a rest. Self-care is an art form that is radical in a world where achievements are valued more than balance.

- How often do you exercise your body? How often do you push its capacity to grow in strength and flexibility?
- Do you avoid daily tasks or life choices to avoid putting in the effort?

Structural Awareness and Systems of Support

Tending to our physical environment and needs also helps us to feel organized mentally and emotionally. Eating regularly, keeping a routine, cleaning your spaces, and organizing areas of your life all help to create a sense of internal balance.

Many people pass up opportunities because they are afraid of or feel overwhelmed. When an opportunity presents itself that calls to your heart, realize that these opportunities are meant for us and our growth. We do not need to miss out on anything. We can create systems to support our dreams and desires. We can call upon our community, adjust our schedules, be creative, and find solutions to participate in all that life brings to us.

Many people believe that there is no support for them, and that the world is pushing against them. If we believe the world is scary and unfriendly, we will create that reality. If we think the world is unforgiving and terrible, it will be. If we think that people will rip us off and danger is around the corner, we will experience that. The emotional charge of fear is a powerful attractor. What we send out, we get back. When we are open to seeing people and the universe as supportive, help comes from all directions.

- What is your relationship with organization and delegation?
- Are you able to ask for support easily?
- Do you have an active support system and community?

Standing Your Ground in the Face of Adversity

There will be times when you will have to face situations that feel like a confrontation. These situations activate a response to fight, run away, or freeze in your tracks. No one else is going to fight our battles for us. We must be ready to stand our ground. When we trust ourselves, we can face challenges and fight for what we want. It is common for spiritually-minded people to think it is more spiritual to be passive. While choosing your battles is wise, we must also be prepared to stand up as an ambassador of Truth and Justice.

- Are you comfortable with asserting boundaries and standing up for yourself?
- What is your relationship with conflict? What are your habitual and historical responses to conflict?

Presence, Faith, and Trust: Everything in Divine Timing

Know that everything is coming at the right time. We are never late. We are always where we need to be in life to get to where we want to go. Trust in the unfolding of your path. If you miss an opportunity and it was truly meant for you, it will come around again.

- Do you feel you have enough time to accomplish your life goals?
- Do you feel patient while also maintaining focus and determination towards your goals?

Belonging: You Belong, So Does Everyone Else

Go out into the world and know that you belong, and so does everybody else. We are all family, distant relatives with varied pasts. We all want the same things, such as love, acceptance, and freedom. These qualities are already available to us if we would only allow them into our experience. Just like a tree, spread your roots far and deep. Be rooted in many places and cultivate many relationships, many levels of connection and support. You matter and should be shared with the world.

- Do you feel you belong? In your family? In your workplace? In your community? On the Earth? How do those beliefs affect how you move in the world?

Illuminated Tree Trunk Meditation

Close your eyes and imagine yourself as a tall and sturdy tree. Feel your roots grow deep and wide into Gaia. Imagine nutrients absorbing up through your roots helping you to feel strong and nourished. If there is any density in your being, allow it to dissolve into the ground through your roots.

Feel your branches growing wide and far towards the heavens. Imagine life force from the universe pouring in through your branches and revitalizing your whole system. You can even allow your tree to flow gently in the wind.

Feel that you are a loving tree that many sweet animals love to come and take refuge in. Imagine that your love is so strong that magical creatures like to come and play around the tree. Radiate this love out into the world.

Feel the other loving trees across the world that are connected to your root system. Feel them pulsing love and strength out into the world. Take a deep, long breath and feel the power of this connection.

Amplify this intention by chanting the sounds of LAM or OM over and over, sending waves of vibration out through your being.

When you are finished, return to normal breathing, and open your eyes.

FOUR

Sacral Chakra: Divine Creatorship

It is said that all our suffering is from a root ignorance of not knowing who we are as divine beings of Pure Consciousness. We falsely believe that we are this body and our limited egoic self. Since we erroneously think we are only this limited self made of flesh and bone, we endlessly chase sensory experiences thinking our happiness will somehow be found in the world. We have created an entire civilization built from this ignorance and suffer greatly because of it.

We are each Source Consciousness reflected as an individual soul appearing to have a temporary physical experience as a human. Once we incarnate, we forget our spiritual legacy and are born into a world of limitations. We become entangled in our identification with our body and mind. We are told our names and given a family identity and history. We live in a community that has a communal identity. We live in a nation that has a certain national identity and ways of behaving. We are told we are human, and even this has certain rules and regulations on behavior and certain limitations. We even extend our identity out into a galactic and universal identity. All these identities are temporary and change with each incarnation. We are not a finite being existing in only one place and time. We are the One Light of Consciousness in which all of Creation appears within.

When we identify as our body, egoic identity, memories, family, emotions, circumstances, our careers, mistakes, and so on, we lose focus on our eternal nature and identify with some passing experience. We cut ourselves off from our Source-ness. Spiritual growth is about aligning with our Divine Nature and remembering the truth of who we are. As we continually refocus ourselves on our Divine Nature and the Light of Source, we transform into an embodiment of Source Energy.

The Sacral Chakra, located in the lower abdomen in line with the sacrum, is all about identity and how we relate to the world around us. Everything is in a relationship. This center is related to creativity and sexuality. It is represented by the water element and connects us to the flow of our vital body, our subtle energy system. It inspires movement and connects with our desires. It shows us what we feel drawn to, what we have aversions to, and if we value ourselves enough to attain our desires.

When we are in a flow state, we are aligned with the energy of creation and are absorbed in the experience of creation. When we are in our knowledge of who we truly are and not wrapped up in our egoic identity, our sexual connections become a technology to experience Source in another through sacred sexual union.

This center gives us the ability to sense our emotions and connects us with the emotional projections of those around us, especially concerning intimacy, sexuality, and desire. We can sense if others are drawn to us or if they are not interested. When people's Sacral Centers are imbalanced, they have difficulty processing emotions and relating to others. This center manifests our ability to move and create in the world. Are we open and free? Do we have limitations and rigid rules of relating?

When this center is balanced, we feel artistic and creative. We are inspired to follow our visions and dreams. We have a charismatic and engaging expression that inspires and uplifts others. We have healthy sexual relationships. We have clear emotional, energetic, and sexual boundaries in our relations. We see ourselves as equal to others and can connect deeply with others and create intimate (sexual and non-sexual) bonds. We enjoy spontaneity and freethinking and are creative problem solvers.

When this center is imbalanced, we may experience a lack of creativity. We may have trouble connecting authentically or creating deep bonds with others. We may sell out on our dreams because we do not feel we can achieve them and instead, follow the money, convenience, and prestige. This may keep us in a state of perpetual longing and an unfulfilled desire for a more purposeful life. We may blame others because we cannot see that our emotional/mental patterns are creating our reality. We may have unhealthy sexual relationships, sexual addictions, and poor emotional, relational, and sexual boundaries. We may blame others and project our emotions onto them. We may be critical and judgmental of others' creativity. We may experience moodiness, pessimism, and apathy. We may be deceitful and manipulative to get our needs met by others.

This could manifest physically as reproductive system issues, sexually transmitted infections, painful or irregular menstrual cycles, erectile dysfunction, lower back pain, bladder problems, and more.

What Imbalances the Sacral Chakra?

Not Meeting Our Own Expectations

Life is full of challenges, and when we experience emotional trauma from perceived failures, we may lose sight of who we are and identify with our mistakes or shortcomings. This causes us to give up on ourselves, and we feel like a failure.

The truth is that life is about learning. Sometimes we hit the mark, and sometimes we fall short. We are not our bodies, thoughts, behaviors, or past actions. Each challenge brings us opportunities to grow, and when we do not meet our expectations for ourselves, we can use the experience to learn. You do not have to change YOU. You simply need to develop new habits and practices.

- Do you have positive or negative self-dialogue with yourself?
- What are your knee-jerk judgments about yourself when you do not meet your own or others' expectations?
- Do you expect failure or success?
- Do you compare yourself with others?
- Do you feel accepted by others?

Self-doubt and low self-worth are common effects of the process of domestication used by our family and our culture. Maybe we were criticized or compared to others growing up. Maybe we were rejected or insulted by others. This also happens when pressure is put on young children to perform a certain way, such as achieving high grades or excelling in sports. Simply, the belief is, "I am not enough."

What people think about you has more to say about them than it has to do with you. You are a unique being with your own set of qualities that make you one of a kind. What really matters is if you accept and unconditionally love yourself. Source loves you. Your Higher Self loves you. Your guides love you just as you are. When you shift your identity to your Divine Nature, self-love is natural because that is what you are. When you love and appreciate yourself, you surround yourself with others who honor and respect you.

- Do you celebrate your uniqueness or feel out of place, not able to fit in?

- When you walk into a room, do you find yourself trying to brace yourself for unpleasant interactions?
- Are you afraid of engaging in conversation with new crowds or people?
- Do you assume that people are judging you?
- Do you feel yourself overcompensating to get attention and love?
- Do you feel like a sinner? Less than worthy?

Unable to Protect Identity or Enforce Boundaries

This happens when we experience abuse of any kind. We may have been overpowered by someone who asserted their will over ours and we experienced defeat. We may have been bullied or singled out, or even cast out from our social circles.

The Sacral Center and the Throat Center are very connected. When you are connected to your Divine Nature, you can easily communicate your boundaries and desires. We need to be able to compassionately establish boundaries and enforce a boundary when it is crossed. You must learn to stand up for yourself and defend your identity, your unique essence. Some people believe that if you genuinely love someone, you will accept any behavior. When we communicate and enforce our boundaries, this allows people to learn how to love us in a way that feels good to us. We do not need to be a doormat for people.

Your parents teach you this lesson the most. When you can express yourself truthfully and transparently to your parents, it will be much easier to accomplish this challenge with others. If you find yourself constantly standing up to others and it falls on deaf ears, honor your soul and find others who are supportive. This is especially true for your family. You can create a new family that loves and honors you completely. The choice is yours, and it always has been.

- Do you find yourself constantly adjusting your behavior to avoid conflict?
- Do you feel you are authentic in your relationships? Are you able to communicate honestly? If not, what are you afraid will happen if you are transparent and honest?

- Do you find yourself staying in relationships that are painful, hoping that eventually they will change their ways and finally love you the way you want?
- Do you communicate and enforce your boundaries swiftly and easily?

Codependency

Codependency is an unhealthy relationship pattern where one person sacrifices their own personal needs for the needs of others. This pattern is often created in childhood when children learn to overlook their own physical, mental, and emotional needs to survive through unhealthy relationships involving addiction, neglect, and abuse.

People with codependency patterns have a distorted perspective of love because they learned that receiving love meant they had to behave in a certain way to receive positive attention. This belief manifests as an unhealthy reliance on people for approval and a sense of value and identity. This expresses as anything "overly," such as being overly apologetic or overly giving as an attempt to manipulate others to feel safe and loved.

Codependency manifests as low self-esteem, people-pleasing, poor boundaries, reactivity, caretaking, control issues, manipulation, dysfunctional communication, perfectionism, external referencing, feelings of emptiness, intense and unstable relationships, obsession, dependency, denial, problems with intimacy, and other characteristics.

When we are dependent emotionally, financially, and physically on others, we cannot feel equal to them, and separation occurs. The same happens if we feel that others are dependent on us.

If we believe that others are dependent on us or we are dependent on others, we are not free to relate to them authentically and often manipulation occurs. Because of this dependency, we may compromise our dreams and beliefs to sustain this ego dynamic.

Interdependence is a healthy relationship pattern where two people are aware of and value the emotional bond between each other and can maintain a strong, clear perspective of individuality while in the dynamics of the relationship. These types of relationships are built on transparency, vulnerability, and trust. Each person takes full responsibility for their own emotional and mental well-being. Each person's autonomy is supported, and everyone can maintain their own values and unique perspectives.

Healing codependency involves becoming aware of the beliefs and patterns that distort our perspective of who we are and all the ways we limit ourselves to manipulate other people into seeing us as loveable or valuable. This involves reorienting how we relate to others, especially the ones closest to us. It is a moment-to-moment process and practice of compassion and self-love.

Realize that everyone is in a partnership, and everyone is equal. Release others from feeling dependent on you and transform dynamics where you feel dependent on others. Empower yourself and others to follow their highest joy. When everyone follows their joy, everyone benefits, and there is an equal exchange between everyone.

- Do you feel overly responsible for other people's lives and well-being?
- Do you make excuses for other people's behavior?
- Do you try to control or manipulate others to get your needs met?
- Do you find yourself seeking revenge for the wrongdoings of others?
- Do you find yourself seeking the approval of others?
- Do you find yourself limiting yourself or holding back out of fear of causing waves?
- Does the thought of ending unhealthy relationships frighten you?
- Do you take on the guilt or embarrassment of others when they behave inappropriately?
- Is it hard for you to say "no" when someone asks for help?

Sexual Trauma

Sexual trauma affects people long after the initial trauma. It can limit how we show up in intimate relationships. Many of my clients experienced sexual trauma as children, causing their sexual expressions to be distorted. Many of these wounds have been caused by men, which causes people to have fears of men and relationships with men. Often these wounds started long ago in other lifetimes and are now being re-experienced so that the person can heal.

We can heal our sexual trauma and develop a healthy relationship with our sexuality. Maybe it happens slowly over time, or maybe it is something that we can accelerate by finding a professional to guide us through the process. Healing is possible, and we can learn how to open the flow of creative sexual energy in a way that helps us feel compassionately connected to our sexuality.

- What is your sexual history from childhood until now?
- What were your first experiences with your sexuality? Did this involve other people? Was it an enjoyable experience?
- What were your parents' beliefs about sexuality? Masturbation? Did those beliefs get passed on to you?
- Do you have religious beliefs around sexuality that consider sex shameful or immoral?
- What are your beliefs around monogamy, polyamory, homosexuality, and bisexuality?
- Do you feel comfortable with your sexuality? How often do you self-pleasure? What are your beliefs about masturbation?
- What are your thoughts and feelings after orgasm?

Rejecting Womanhood or Manhood

A lot of pressure is put on women to look and behave in certain ways. Some women end up subconsciously hating their womanhood and repressing their feminine qualities. A lot of men are insecure about the size of their penis or body structure and feel that they are not "manly" enough. Some people do not feel that they fit into a binary gender system. All these issues can distort how we express ourselves in the world.

Everyone can feel sexy. Everyone can feel attractive. Everyone has what it takes to be a good lover. Sexiness and beauty are feelings that we can generate in ourselves. We can learn to be connected and confident lovers. Accept that you have masculine and feminine qualities that contribute to your own unique balance. Neither needs to be repressed, and both can be celebrated.

What are your beliefs around your womanhood/manhood or about your masculinity or femininity (regardless of biological sex)? What does it mean to be a man or a woman? What qualities and responsibilities do men and women have in society? When is it acceptable to show emotion? Do you fit into that model? How can you celebrate your masculine and feminine qualities? Do you find yourself repressing one or the other or both? How do you compare yourself to others of the same sex? Opposite sex? Do you hold judgment about transgenders?

What If You Don't Believe in Relationships?

We may have become closed to intimacy and closeness if we experienced our parents fighting growing up or if they are separated or divorced. We may have experienced the tragic loss or death of a loved one at some point in our life. We may not have had good examples of the sweetness that is possible in close relationships. Maybe we were hurt by others and closed ourselves to love.

In each moment, we have an opportunity to open ourselves to love and align with our Divine Essence. As we learn to trust connection and affection from others, we begin to move more freely in the world. When we learn to be vulnerable and connect with others, we open to the abundance of the universe.

- Are you open to intimate bonds, or do you find yourself hiding your true desires and soul expression?
- Are you open to sexual connections, either with your partner or others? What do you do when your sexual energy activates? Do you repress it? Feel shame? Deny it?
- What thoughts or beliefs drive your aversions or desires?
- What are your beliefs about dating and marriage? Who were your models for relationships growing up?

Fear of Impending Doom

If we are afraid that danger lurks around every corner or that the world is a scary place, this affects how we show up in the world and limits our creative expression. When we focus on the darkness of humanity and the darkness of the world, we miss out on the sweetness that life has to offer. As we learn to trust and build open and honest relationships, we blossom and start to feel safe and secure. Everything is in a relationship, and in every moment, we can choose to be in acceptance and expect goodness, or we can choose resistance and expect to suffer.

- Do you expect your future to be positive or negative?
- Do you find yourself "waiting for the other shoe to drop?"

Sacral Center Meditation

Close your eyes and begin to breathe consciously and deeply. Bring your awareness to your pelvis. If you would like, you can make a triangle with your thumbs and index fingers touching. Bring the triangle to rest so that your index fingers rest on your pubic bone and your thumbs touch close to the belly button. Your palms will gently rest on your lower abdomen. Breathe into this place and imagine that it is filling with light. Fill every part of your pelvic bowl with the light of your awareness. If there is any stagnant or distorted energy in your pelvic bowl, imagine that you can clear it with the light of your loving awareness. Feel your sexual organs. Imagine that you are filling your sexual organs with Divine Light and Love.

Let any negative energy or thoughts fall away as you bring light into your sexual organs. Continue breathing like this for a few minutes. You can chant the words VAM or OM to amplify the healing. When you're finished, return to normal breathing, and open your eyes.

FIVE

Conscious Relating & Sacred Sexuality

From the moment we are born, we absorb our family and culture's thought forms and belief systems. Many of us are taught that the body is shameful, and that sexuality is dirty and disgraceful. We project those values out into the world and pass them along to the next generations. These limiting beliefs are like a wet blanket put over the light of our soul, restricting the free-flowing brilliance of creative pleasure.

Sexual wounding and dysfunction are held by all of us. We deny and repress our innate drives for connection and pleasure, which fractal out into a myriad of dysfunctional and self-serving behaviors that can harm ourselves and others. Over the coming years, we will be invited to hold space for all the collective healing regarding sexuality and how we connect intimately.

Intimacy and sexuality are two different qualities bodymind experience. In modern society, they are often confused as the same. I wrote this section to bring deeper awareness to what intimacy is and what sexuality is, and how we can grow and mature in both areas.

Intimate Relationships

Intimate relationships can be measured by how many areas of life we are open to sharing with someone and how deep into those areas we are comfortable growing in that relationship. Some relationships are superficial and practical, like an exchange between people in a grocery store, and some relationships involve sharing a wide variety of experiences and going deep into one's heart like with a parent or a life partner.

A lot of people experience their sexuality from an animalistic and service-to-self impulse. Some use sexuality to control, manipulate, or dominate others to fulfill their own desires and fantasies. Some repress and deny their sexual desires to fit into societal structures of "purity" to cover up their own shame and guilt.

Sexuality in its highest form is for the cultivation of Divine Light and Union with the Divine. In the highest form, sexuality uses our body temple, senses, and creative power to connect with and channel our divine nature's pleasure.

Divine Partnership and Twin Flame Relationships

As we grow spiritually, we release the control and manipulation patterns of the old and open to true partnership. In Spiritual Partnership, each person is seen as an equal, and the bond is used as a technology for spiritual growth. Any relationship can be a spiritual partnership. In spiritual partnership, both people take responsibility for their own emotional and mental well-being.

Twin Flame relationships are a major phenomenon on the planet right now. As many are finishing their soul's karmic contracts, they are now ready to meet their Divine Mirror. In Twin Flame relationships, each partner is committed to serving the other on their path of healing and feels that their relationship is meant to serve the collective of humanity.

Twin Flame relationships are examples of true Divine Union and create a new model for relationships on the planet based on transparency, unconditional love, and planetary service. These "power couples" work through the last of their conditionings together, the last of their unprocessed emotional trauma, and exemplify cooperative collaboration in its highest human form. Many Twin Flames are now finishing up their purging and activation phases and embodying Divine Androgyny, also called *Heiros Gamos* by some in the ascension community.

I felt it was important to note the "spiritual trap" of the term "Twin Flame" in the ascension community. In many ways, the old models of relating have been superimposed on the pathway of divine partnership where people are "on the hunt" for their Twin Flame. People use the word "Twin Flame" as a control and manipulation tactic just like some who use the term "I love you" to guilt others into playing a role for them. Some feel like they aren't ascending or somehow have less value if they do not have a Twin Flame relationship. I must say, I am in a Twin Flame relationship, and we hardly ever call each other that. We do not label ourselves in that way because it can create control structures. We do not use the term to say, "Now that we are Twin Flames, we cannot do this, and we have to do that." True divine partnership is finding union within one's deepest self which is supported by and reflected by the other but is never dependent on the other person. That power is in the individual.

Divine Androgyny: Balancing Masculine & Feminine

The fabric of nature is woven by feminine and masculine principles engaged in an eternal dance of creation and evolution. We experience this Law of Gender through the two sexes of our species and the expression of gender. We depart from the classroom of polarized gender and move into an exalted state of androgyny when we embody more of a balanced embodiment of masculine and feminine qualities. We see this outpictured as women come into places of power and men come into the softness of their hearts.

Pre-Life Contracts on Sexuality

Before incarnating on the Earth, we choose how we are going to explore sexuality in our life. Some choose to be attracted to bodies of the same sex; some choose to be attracted to members of the opposite sex; and some choose to be attracted to both. The truth is everyone falls somewhere on the spectrum of attracted-to-same or attracted-to-opposite, and the placement on that spectrum fluctuates over time.

Non-Traditional Gender Expression

Many young people do not feel connected to a binary gender system and feel that their gender expression and sexuality are much more fluid compared to the mainstream model. These forerunners of consciousness not only bring in a new embodiment to the Earth School, but they also help us to evolve the old belief systems of judgment and bigotry into a higher unity of the heart.

I believe that as we clear limiting beliefs and trauma, we will all become more gender-fluid and open to more levels of intimacy, touch, and sexual expression. It is up to each of us to do the inner work to heal the wounds of our past regarding sexuality and learn to embody our unique expression of sexual truth.

These times are challenging for those who are bringing in this new energy and new embodiment. Many of these beings have never been in a physical body, let alone a body that has a specific sex. Some of these souls come from star systems where they have only lived in androgynous forms. Some have lived in opposite expressions many times and wanted to try the opposite in this incarnation to learn balance. Some needed the experience of being "different" so they would awaken quicker to their starseed origins.

The challenge and invitation are for these unique souls to make a home within their bodies and make peace with themselves in the world. It is a noble challenge that bears much fruit. These beings, especially the new children, cannot be defined by labels of any kind in terms of gender and sexuality. Each being is unique and beautiful! Imagine how powerful their souls must be to come at such a time and face such judgment and ridicule only to use it to awaken in their consciousness. They are truly changemakers!

The prototype for this new energy was a child of Yeshua ben Joseph and Mary Magdalene. A high-vibration androgynous being was born into the new crystalline bloodline created by Jesus and Mary to test out the biology's capacity to hold such a powerful soul. This intersexed child, having both male and female reproductive organs, was trained in the esoteric arts and on the path of mastery and awakening. I cannot even begin to imagine how empowered this being was considering his parents were cosmic tantric illuminated masters!

We are invited to grow in compassion and understanding and support those of the two-spirited, transgendered expression to embody the magic that they already are and assist them on their path of discovery who they are beyond their bodymind. They are divine and perfect as they are! Having this beautiful, rainbow expression of gender and sexuality marks a renaissance of love across this planet.

Everyone is being invited into their sexual truth to explore their deepest, most soulful erotic expression. Each person is invited to expand their concepts regarding relationships and sexuality. We have so much love to give and receive! Let us help one another come into profound, intimate union with our deepest selves and celebrate our creative spirit! May all wounds around sexuality and our body be healed now and forever!

Sacred Touch

Many people are starved for true, loving affection in their life. Sacred touch is experienced as a loving, conscious physical interaction between two or more people where there is an honoring of each person's divinity. When we hold hands, we can invite the Divine to be with us. When we hug one another, we can invite the presence of the Light to move through us and wrap us in a loving embrace. We can invite the Divine into all our connections and relationships to lift us up into a higher experience of Love and Unity.

We, as a collective, confuse intimacy and touch as sexuality. This confusion keeps us from experiencing a deep, loving connection with one another. There are even different cultural rules and limitations depending on people's sex and gender. We have so many rules and regulations of how we should interact with one another that it leaves many feeling alone and disconnected from their community.

I see this strongly in male relationships. Men have been programmed to believe that sharing a loving touch or an embrace shows weakness or somehow reflects their sexuality or status in a negative way. Many men are completely deprived of non-sexual physical intimacy. On a deep level, men are deprived of a true sense of brotherhood and intimate connection because of this. Distorted programs around sexuality, touch, and intimacy are so deeply embedded in male-embodied beings that we see a huge amount of suffering created in the world by men. Many men turn to drugs, alcohol, closeted sexuality, sexual abuse, and even suicide as a symptom of this distortion and deficiency.

As we normalize loving touch and consensual embraces across sexes and genders, we will see less and less perversion in human sexuality as a collective. As we embody higher sexual honesty and celebrate our sensuality and sexuality, we clear the past generations' distortions and protect future generations from sexual trauma and repression.

Relationship Models

Old relationship models passed on from previous generations and religious institutions are often experienced as systems of control based on fear and dogma. Some traditions view women as the property of men. Jealousy is seen by some as a sign of "true love," and women are taught to be servants to their husbands, relinquishing their own sovereignty to fulfill the needs and desires of their husbands. Some cultures force the younger generations to secure public image and familial financial legacy. In many ways, marriage has become a hunting act, where people are chasing the person they think will complete them or make them happy. People copy the manipulation tactics from television to coerce people into staying in relationships much longer than is healthy because of public image, fear of the unknown, guilt, and low self-worth.

I know for myself, as a gay male, I had to come to terms with the fact that I would not be following the traditional model. I had to do much inner work to deconstruct the belief systems passed on of what it means to be a man, a son, and a lover. There was so much trauma, conditioning, and secrecy to work through. I had to learn how to live an authentic and joyful life publicly as a male who is only attracted to men. It was extremely painful but was the only way for me to truly live a happy life and have honest relationships with others. We all have sexual and relating karma to clear and as we heal ourselves, we heal the future generations as well.

These old models limit authentic behavior and expression of humanity and keep people trapped within their relationships. New Earth relationship models honor the free-will sovereignty of each individual. Instead of controlling our partners, we empower them to follow their intuition and path to grow. Instead of making assumptions and placing expectations on one another and the relationship, we choose to grow in the ability to communicate our needs, desires, and limitations honestly and with full transparency. Instead of blaming others for our experience, we take emotional responsibility and use conflict to learn and grow into maturity and compassion.

Monogamy is the choice to explore sexual energy cultivation and deep intimate emotional bonds with a single partner. Non-monogamy is when someone chooses to practice relating beyond the dyadic relationship structure of monogamy. Within non-monogamy are a few different categories of relationship styles. Some people identify as polyamorous and feel open to multiple romantic and/or sexual relationships or may practice polyfidelity where they are committed to multiple partners. Some people choose to have a primary relationship where they have consensually agreed-upon commitments and secondary partners that they engage with on certain levels which could be sexual, romantic, or both. Open relationships are becoming more of a trend in the younger generations who wish to create new relating structures; this is especially true amongst the gay male population. Couples may engage sexually with other couples, "swinging," or be mostly monogamous with certain degrees of outside sexual or romantic engagement at certain times in their life. Some call this being "monogamish." These diverse relationship styles require conscious communication, transparency, and honesty to work and are not for everyone. They require one to be willing to work on themselves and grow in sovereignty or else things can get dramatic quickly!

Inherently, life is polyamorous, but we may choose to focus our time and emotional/energetic investment on one single partnership for any duration of time. This does not mean that once in a relationship, either of the partners should deny or repress their natural human attraction to other humans. The energy of attraction and arousal is natural, and we should work with it in healthy ways within whatever relationship styles and structures we currently practice.

Everyone is free to create relationship structures that support their spiritual growth, joy, and freedom. While non-monogamy and polyamorous relationship styles are growing in popularity, it is important to intend that all of our relationships be focused on mutual growth and love. No one should be forced into being monogamous out of fear and control. No one should be polyamorous or in a non-monogamous relationship if that does not support their higher vision for their life and their level of comfort. Monogamy is beautiful and should be respected just as much as the non-monogamy styles. What matters is that love, compassion, integrity, honesty, and the willingness to refine one's inner world are present in all relationship styles.

Conscious Communication

Conscious relationships involve clear and honest communication. When we utilize our relationships for spiritual growth, we acknowledge when we are afraid, insecure, or jealous. Instead of controlling our partners so that we feel comfortable and perpetuate patterns of limitation, we can communicate our fears and doubts and transform our fearful parts into true and authentic empowerment and freedom. The highest form of communication is to set the other free. Deep listening and nonviolent communication pave the way to freedom and joy for all.

Compassionate Listening: Setting Intention

Compassionate listening means that we have emptied our mind and simply rest in the intention of relieving the suffering of another through deep listening. As we listen to the other person and practice compassionate listening, we do not plan what we will say next. We notice when we want to jump into the conversation and choose to stay in simple, mindful awareness of the one who is sharing while being deeply anchored in inner presence and breath.

Triggered Reactive Emotion

As someone shares the story of their suffering, their body re-experiences the traumatic energy so that it can be released. You may start to feel the same feelings and sensations that they do, or it may trigger your own trauma stored in the body. When you are aware of this, take a deep breath, connect with your Pillar of Light, the hara line, and re-establish your alignment with your Higher Self. As you exhale, release the energy that is triggered and unsettled within you. This also helps the other person become aware of and release their triggered energy. As you clear, they clear, and both of you feel the support of your shared conscious awareness. This light structure meditation is talked about in *pranamaya kosha* section of this book.

Body Language & Guiding Self-Inquiry

For some, moving from irrational thoughts and painful emotions takes a little more time. Notice the posture, micro-muscle movement in the face, dilation of the pupils, and breathing patterns of the person sharing. Body language tells a lot about what a person is going through internally. Asking questions helps them go deeper into their feelings, thoughts, and sensations so that they can get to the core of the issue and understand the deeper nature of the conflict. You may notice them tensing up as they share their perspective as their body and mind re-experiences the pain. Ask them what they feel as they share their story. Contractions or activating energy in the body point to the chakra where the limiting belief and stored trauma are held. When we tune into that part of the body and practice compassionate listening with our Inner Being, we can uncover valuable information for transformation and healing.

Internal Imagery Mindfulness

We are constantly broadcasting mental imagery out into the Unified Field. Every fluctuation of thought sends packets of data into the field that can be picked up by others. For most people, this happens unconsciously. As we awaken and become aware of our internal processes and intentions, we become deliberate creators. We begin to choose our thoughts and create our future from an inspired vision versus creating from our past memories, trauma, and conditioned thinking.

When we are thinking of or talking with someone, we are broadcasting imagery in their direction that they are filtering through their energy system through their subconscious. When we are listening to another, we are receiving imagery and energy from them as they share.

Notice your internal messaging and images you receive while listening and be mindful of the images you project. While the other is sharing, you can hold an internal image of what it would be like when they are transformed by love. As you hold this internal image, your subconscious begins to pick up on this broadcast. Depending on the amount of internal resistance occurring, their subconscious picks up the data and begins to signal to the conscious mind to match the higher frequency and ease.

Refocusing and Regrounding

If you notice that a person is getting unfocused or holding a lot of tension, you can guide them through your own ability to stay connected to your higher consciousness and grounded beingness. Sometimes people unconsciously disassociate and drift away to avoid feeling the pain of what they are going through. Helping them come back into their body with deep, conscious breathing empowers them to face the issue with mindfulness and confidence. Sometimes people drift off because they have lost interest in their own stories. If you start to feel unsettled in yourself, you are likely absorbing their energy and mental imagery. Breathe consciously, connect with your hara line, strengthen your field, and settle into your heart.

As you ground your energy, the other person unconsciously receives the messaging from your broadcast, which can activate grounding and presence in them.

Triggering and Venting

If the person sharing vents in your direction, it is important not to take it personally. What you are witnessing is them tapping into the original wound that happened way before your conversation, sometimes lifetimes ago. Get curious, not furious. Take a deep breath and clear the energy that may have been triggered in you from their projected suffering. Breathe into your whole spine and heart. Do your absolute best to clear any energy within you that may come from a place of needing to defend yourself. Let them know that you see that they are suffering and care for them. Practice mirroring and asking questions that lead to deeper answers.

Validation, Feedback, and Mirroring

For many, being heard is enough for them to release deeply embedded suffering. Repeating back what you heard in your own words helps the person sharing feel heard and understood. What was at "the heart" of what they shared? Once you have repeated back what you understood and heard, you can ask if you missed anything. If you have missed an important detail, let them share what you missed and repeat it back to them to make sure you have touched on every part of their perspective. It does not matter if what they are saying is accurate. What matters is that they feel heard and validated.

If you have insight into the nature of their suffering, try asking questions to help them come up with the answer themselves. Ask questions that help them feel and see clearly. This empowers them to be their own healer, their own redeemer.

When someone shares from a vulnerable place, it is important to validate their experience so that they can feel safe enough to release the energy completely. You can say something like, "I see how painful that was and still is for you. Would you like to take a deep breath together and let some of that energy go?" This willingness to feel the pain instead of running from it is often enough to make a significant shift in their perspective and health as well as builds a deeper bond between the sharer and the compassionate listener.

Advice

I find it is most beneficial to help others discover deeper levels of truth within themselves before offering advice. Many people have walls of resistance that come up when they feel like they are "being told what to do" or when someone seems to think they are "better than them." Using mirroring and compassionate inquiry can help avoid running into this wall.

Before giving anything that may sound like advice, ask if you can share your perspective. Honor their "yes" or their "no." If they say yes, let them know they can take what is helpful and disregard the rest. When sharing, use "I" statements. "When I went through _____, I discovered that _____. Do you feel this relates to your experience? Is that helpful at all? If so, how could you apply this to your life?"

Reframing

We often frame the experience of a traumatic experience through the lens of victimhood and limited perception. "Reframing" helps us understand the traumatic event from a higher perspective, which opens the pathways to healing and redemption. Reframing moves us out of the experience of victim mentality into a higher understanding of how the situation served our soul's evolution.

Envisioning the Ideal Circumstances

So often, people create their NOW and future based on their past experiences and traumas. We can climb out of that lower trajectory by creating an inspired vision of what we would like to manifest in the most ideal ways. We can help our community members to do the same so that we all collectively envision a higher trajectory for ourselves, our community, and our planetary civilization.

Agreements in Conscious Relationships

Within the structure of any pairing, monogamous or non-monogamous, agreements are made consciously and unconsciously about what actions and behaviors are acceptable while in the container of the relationship. Conscious relating evolves us out of assumed gender roles and societal norms and into unique connections that honor each individual's sovereign creation. Agreements can be made on sharing resources, sexual intimacy, household duties, responsibilities, when time is spent together, when time is spent with other people, when time is spent alone, and so on.

High Sexuality: High Alchemy

The highest form of sexual activity is for the attainment of higher consciousness and union with the Divine. Old systems of sexuality are control systems that describe when, how, if, and with whom a person can participate in a sexual act. These systems will fall away as more and more people become aware of the ascension technology that is activated by sexual pleasure.

I would like to propose that sex falls in the spectrum between service-to-self and service-to-all where the lowest forms involve violence and domination, and the highest forms involve heartfelt service, pleasure, connection, and devotion.

When someone is aroused sexually, creative life force energy begins to move through the body's electric and magnetic fields as it prepares to create new energy and, ultimately, new life. All the best energy of one's being is offered up from the cells and endocrine system as the body prepares to create a new life. This process happens much faster and more powerfully when two or more people are engaged in sexual touch and play.

At the core of sacred sexuality is self-love. This is not an egoic worshipping of yourself but a compassionate and caring attitude towards your being. Loving another as you love yourself requires you to love your own body, mind, and Spirit first. When we deeply love ourselves, we naturally and effortlessly radiate that love out into the world.

Cultivation

Cultivating sexual energy charges the body with powerful healing and transformative energy. When circulated and anchored properly, sexual energy cultivation improves creativity, focus, mood, and our relationship to the world around us. In ancient times, the priests and priestesses would cultivate sexual energies and anchor them into the collective field of their community to raise the collective's creative potential. Everyone benefits when individuals are trained in the high alchemy of heart-based, sexual energy cultivation.

Self-Pleasure and Self-Cultivation

When you activate your own sexual, creative energies, you can circulate the energies to heal the body with self-love and pleasure. Stroke and caress the skin of your body to activate the electromagnetic fields. Explore the sensitive erogenous areas of the body like nipples, perineum, and genitals. Use deep, conscious breathing to amplify the electric and magnetic waves of energy that begin to flow through you as you begin to charge the body. Circulate the energies by doing the microcosmic orbit, alternate nostril breathing, or other conscious breathing patterns to bring the energies up the spine and spread them throughout your whole body. Imagine that all your cells are illuminating and being healed as you spread this light through your systems.

Multi-orgasmic Men

Many men around the world are lost in the shadows of sexual addiction and porn industry programming that focuses on assertiveness and ejaculation. Many men are beginning to tune into the sexual arts to heal these toxic patterns and distortions in their sexuality. I highly recommend the work of Mantak Chia.

A male orgasm is made of two physical responses. One is the explosion of orgasmic power, and the second is ejaculation. Ejaculation uses a considerable amount of life force energy. While it may be exciting and pleasurable to experience, ejaculating immediately creates a depletion in energy. Using different tantric practices, men can learn how to control their sexual energy to have multiple orgasms without ejaculating.

Another level of sexual growth for the majority of men is the feminine quality of lovemaking. The Divine Feminine in a male form is what makes them a good lover. The softness, receptivity, gentleness, and care are what moves men out of porn sex and into the higher arts of sexual alchemical wizardry and noble kingship!

Womb Magic

Within the female womb is a powerful energy portal that allows the passage of a soul from the Higher Realms to the Earth matrix. Priestesses would use this vortex to channel energies into the Earth plane for healing and rejuvenation. Ancient priestesses would use the power of stem cells in their menstrual blood to heal and strengthen food crops and regenerate the Earth.

Womb-en all around the world are healing their sexual trauma and celebrating the power of their sexuality. Lifetimes and generations of trauma are stored in the womb and are ready to be transformed and healed. Sister Circles, Goddess Temples, and Red Tent spaces create healthy containers for *womb-en* to tune into the power and wisdom of their wombs.

The following is a short transcription from an IQH session with a somnambulistic client named Emma's Higher Self.

M: I am wondering if you have any final messages for Ron and me?

HS: There is a new movement — you are talking about it quietly. You are not sure how to bring it out into the open because of certain taboos, but it is going to be a great part of empowering others. Once you release certain boundaries, you don't notice the programming of sexuality is heavy. These practices help you to listen fully and walk through the door.

M: What's the movement that you speak about?

HS: Bodies. Many pleasuring together. Shameless. Love. Trust. Vulnerability is power. Everything at once. Pure.

M: So, are you speaking about sexual liberation?

HS: Sexual truth.

M: And how is sexual truth important in our lives or on our path?

HS: The barriers are always made up of small denials. We deny our powerlessness. We deny our power. We deny our now. We call shame to our impulses, and we cry havoc to our words. We stuff them down — all of it tied in a ball — weighted down — keep it earthbound.

M: So, what role do we have in this movement? What do our souls have to do in these bodies regarding this movement?

HS: Once you find the right words, you will feel more comfortable about broadening, but you are going to collect more souls that agree. It has already begun. Just remember, they are not your shape (energy signature), and so you cannot relate to them in the same way that you have been related to. You must speak and leave it for others to own in their own way. And in that way, even though it will be a great and easy thing to do, you will continue to stay humble and not fall into an ego trip because this is going to be intoxicating.

M: Intoxicating in what way?

HS: To power centers.

Introductory Tantric Practices

Tantric practices use the mind and intention to move subtle energy through the body for healing and awakening. Here are some basic skills that one can use to deepen their relationship to their sexuality or connect more deeply with another.

Breath Awareness

When we are aroused, our heart rate and breathing become erratic as the pleasure rises in our being. Learning to be mindful of the stages of breathing and expanding each phase of a breath cycle helps to control sexual energy. For example, as men approach orgasmic climax, their breathing becomes shorter and faster. Extending and equalizing the breath stages helps to control ejaculation so that orgasms can be extended, multiplied, and amplified without needing to ejaculate.

Visualization

Learning how to visualize the movement of energy in your own body helps to direct the energy to where it is needed. Sexual life force can be directed into various organs, tissues, chakras, energy pathways, and so on to promote healing and expansion. You can also use visualization and intention to direct energy through your partner's body and energetic field to develop a deeper connection and provide healing energy to your partner.

Spinal Awareness

When we activate sexual energy, it is important to direct the energy out of the genitals, up the spine, and into the rest of the body. This will help awaken the pleasure centers in the body, unblock pathways of energy, and prolong and amplify orgasmic power. The most commonly used technique is the Microcosmic Orbit from Traditional Chinese Medicine. Various meditation and breathing practices are found in the chapters to help circulate and cultivate vital, subtle energy.

Guidance for Connecting with Another

Sexual Attraction

When we connect our sexuality with our sacred hearts, we desire an intimate connection with those we are sexually attracted to. There is nothing shameful about sexual attraction to other people. What we do with the energy and the intention behind our actions is what is important. Sacred sexuality puts love, compassion, and free-will choice at the forefront of any sexual interaction.

Voice Your Attraction

Talking with someone about your attraction to them can be uncomfortable, and it can also open the door for deeper intimacy and transparency. If you feel chemistry with someone, you can voice your attraction if it feels appropriate. Once you voice your attraction, you can listen to their response and see if the other person feels the same. Much suffering happens for people due to unrequited love and unrecognized longing.

Consent is Sexy

With consent, there are no grey areas. "Yes" means yes. "No" means no, and "maybe" means NO.

Often people engage in sex with partners they do not want to connect with. Notice body language, yours and theirs, and honor your perceptions. If you notice discomfort or resistance in yourself or another, honor that. Be vocal and communicate what you are noticing. This may start a transformative conversation for both of you that results in a deeper intimate bond.

Setting a Container

If someone is interested in exploring a deeper way of relating with you, you can set a container together for how you will proceed. This may look like talking more, scheduling a date, cuddling, or sharing deeper levels of affection. If the connection moves towards sexual energy cultivation, talk about what you like in advance so that everyone knows each other's boundaries. This is especially important if you will be exploring parts of sexuality that one or either of you has never explored before, such as someone who has never been with someone of the same sex or has not been sexual with someone in a long time or never at all.

Stages of Sexual Play

Cultivating sexual energy alone or with a partner(s) can be broken into three sections. Foreplay, building to a climax, and what can be called cocooning.

Conscious Multidimensional Foreplay

Before we begin to activate sexual energies, each individual can take a moment to connect with their own heart and breath. Conscious and complete breathing that utilizes the lower and upper abdomen creates a container of awareness to observe and utilize subtle energy. If you are connecting with another, take a moment to synchronize breathing, and look into each other's eyes. Use foreplay to open the senses and activate the subtle energies of yourself and your partner. Stroking the skin with a light touch and gentle kisses activate pleasure sensations in the body and open the body for more powerful energy experiences and awareness.

Building the Orgasmic Waves

As the energy builds, allow it to ebb and flow in several ranges and arcs of pleasure. Tune into the sexual energies of yourself and your partner. Communicate what your partner can do to increase your pleasure and feel more connected. Let your partner know when something is uncomfortable or when you feel disconnected.

Allow yourself to enjoy the experience fully. Use your mind to visualize the movement of energy up the spine and throughout the whole body while staying in conscious connection with your partner and your own breathing. You can use your eyes, body, and breath to direct your partners' energy as well, healing them as you generate love and pleasure. Continue to deepen and elongate the breath to keep from rushing over the edge of pleasure.

As you climax, direct the energy up the back of the spine, arching the energy over the crown and back down the front of the body into the heart. Circulate this energy using the microcosmic orbit to ankh the energy in an infinite loop of pleasure sensations up the back of the spine and down the front of the body.

Cocooning in Radiance

After the climax phase(s), spend time cocooning in the energy cultivated with yourself and your partner(s). Breathe this potent energy into the cells of the body, recharging them with vital energy. Guide the energies back to a grounded place with light kisses and loving touch and rest in the radiance you have created.

Take time to talk about what you liked and what could have made the experience more enjoyable. This helps both of you become more connected and conscious lovers. It may also get the energies flowing again for more play.

However you choose to explore your sexuality, do it with Divine Love. Sex was meant to bring us closer to our True Self, closer to our partners, and closer to Source. Having positive sexual perspectives and experiences is a sign of spiritual maturity. Release all shame connected to your body and your sexuality and embrace the powerful, sexual, creative being that you are.

By healing your own layers of shame and sexual trauma, you help heal our ancestors and future generations, which is an honorable and noble act of service.

My Wedding Vows

I have decided to share my wedding vows that I wrote when Ron and I made our sacred agreement to unite our paths in front of friends, family, and the presence of the Divine. I made these agreements in a way that empowered both of us to live an interdependent and loving relationship. We wanted our marriage to be used as an ascension technology to liberate our consciousness and the consciousness of our beloved. Feel free to use these vows for your own sacred ceremony or create your own.

Ron, my beloved partner,

My heart has been searching for its true love for many years, possibly even many lifetimes. I know that this longing search has truly been a search to find myself. I am the one that I search for. You are my mirror, map, and compass, always reflecting back to me and directing me to the Truth of Who I Am.

I vow to remind you that you are also an extension of Source Energy and that your existence on this planet is far more important than any of us could ever imagine. I encourage you to boldly follow your excitement, filling all that you do with your Light.

I vow to take full responsibility for my own emotional well-being. I will not be dependent on you for happiness and will instead work vigilantly on transforming my own seeds of anger, jealousy, pride, and so forth into a garden of compassion and bliss.

I vow to use my gift of language and speech in the most conscious way, being a poet of honesty and loving-kindness. I do this so that you know the depth of my love for you and this life we are creating together.

I vow to practice non-violence in thought and action and to honor the body as the sacred temple of your soul and divine nature. I promise never to touch you in a way that does not benefit our independent and mutual spiritual development.

I vow to take care of this planet and all its intricate and beautiful forms of life. I vow to be in constant service to the Greater Good, for I know that I am of Source Energy just as much as the trees and stars. If we are blessed to have the gift of children, I want them to experience the beauty that this world has to offer, just as we have.

I love you as I love myself. I vow to align myself with my highest vibration, following my soul's true excitement. It is my hope that as I continue to radiate my love for myself that you will always be inspired to align yourself with all that excites and nourishes your soul. I vow to give you the fullest me that I can.

SIX

Solar Plexus Chakra:
Divine Willpower

True power comes when we are aligned with our Divine Self. Our Divine Self is like the Sun of our Solar System. It is bright, powerful, and independent. It remains shining even if clouds cover our perception of it. It continues shining even if someone curses at it and says that it is too bright. Even if we are in emotional turmoil, our True Nature is there shining eternally. We are each the center of our own universe. If we truly want to feel powerful, we must be like the Sun and align with our True Nature and shine out into the world.

Our Solar Plexus Chakra, our Power Center, is the home of our willpower and personal strength, is located in the upper abdomen, and is associated with the color orange. It is connected to the element of fire and to the mental body which we access through self-inquiry and mindfulness.

The Solar Plexus gives us the ability to act independently. When this center is balanced, we can face any challenging circumstance without a sense of perfectionism. We take a role of leadership without overpowering, forcing, or dominating others. When we are asked to go out of our comfort zone, we are confident and able to accept the challenge and grow through the experience. In fact, we are likely excited about the opportunity to expand into greater mastery! We can digest the beliefs and opinions of others without needing to make them wrong. We can process our own beliefs and opinions with ownership. We feel calm and collected, residing in our purpose and clear intention.

When this center is imbalanced, we may associate personal power as being bad or unholy. We may become doormats and let others do as they wish, giving our power over to them to make them happy. We may magnetize people to us that confirm our powerlessness and seek the approval of others. We may feel victimized, complaining about how life is never working out for us. We may feel unstable and unable to take control of the circumstances of our life. We may feel reactive, pushy, passive, defeated, frozen, trapped, lethargic, make excuses, or be demanding, controlling, manipulative, and so on.

Imbalances in the Solar Center manifest as digestive system imbalances. We may not be able to process foods and toxins easily. We may find our digestive system is overactive and too hot or underactive and stagnant. We may develop ulcers and cancers as anger eats away at our tissues and cells as well as have other issues in our liver, kidneys, and other digestive organs.

This center is connected to the mind and processes our own thoughts as well as the thoughts and projections of others. This is where we get the phrase, "I can't stomach to even think about it!"

What Imbalances the Solar Plexus?

Dependency, Real or Imagined

If we feel that we are dependent on anyone or anything, we give our power to it. This includes physical, financial, emotional, and mental dependency. While dependency in the Sacral Chakra is about how we feel and emotionally relate, dependency in the Solar Plexus Chakra manifests as our actions, will, and intentions. These two centers are intrinsically related and connected.

Dependency can manifest as manipulative patterns where we behave a certain way to get what we want, or we allow other people to do as they wish out of fear that they will take something from us. It can also manifest as an excessive force when we try to overpower another's will to get them to follow our will. We can feel dependent on our spouse, our career, community, substances, and more.

Dependency causes us to lose track of our own inspired vision and become pessimistic. We may feel that we are always asking for favors and giving our power away in the process. We can also feel and manifest circumstances where others are dependent on us. This gives us a false sense of importance and can keep us from being honest with ourselves and others. It also disempowers the others who feel dependent on us.

Remember that everything is a partnership and that everyone is equal. There is a natural give and take in healthy relationships, an interdependence. We do not need to take responsibility for others' experiences and well-being. We can trust our ability to manifest what we want and empower others to create their own path and to own their creations.

- Where do you believe you are dependent on your parents? Spouse? Government? Parents? Job? Employer? Children? God? This can be financial, situational, emotional, and so on.
- Is that true? How can you adjust your perspective or behavior to exercise and affirm your sovereignty? Your ability to be self-regulated and self-sufficient?

True Consent

Yes means yes. No Means no. Maybe means no! When someone asks something of you, take personal inventory and feel if it aligns with your path and is resonant with your Inner Being. Everyone is familiar with the confusing feeling when your internal realm is in a conflict between your own personal decision of what is best for you and taking care of others' needs. When we feel rushed or pressured, we give our power away. If you are unsure, wait and gather more data to make a sure and clear decision.

- On a scale from 1-10, to what degree are you honoring your internal compass?
- Why might you give in to someone else's needs or requests when they are not a match to the truth of your Inner Being? What beliefs support that behavior?

Empower Others to Be Independent

Empowering others to exercise their free will releases them from patterns of dependency. Release them to follow their highest joy. When we empower others to follow their own intuition and inner knowing, they will blossom, and everyone will benefit. Encourage others to be who they are and to form their own opinions and beliefs.

Drama Triangle: Perpetrator, Rescuer, Victim

Stephen Karpman, MD created a simple tool to understand the patterns of social conflict in relationships. The triangle includes three entry points: Rescuer, Perpetrator, and Victim. These roles have roots in our family of origin, and everyone has a habitual entry position. While people may jump from seat to seat in a conversation, eventually everyone ends up in the

Victim position unless they are able to return to their sovereign self and take full ownership of their creation.

- Where does drama play out in your relationships?
- How do you create the conditions consciously and unconsciously?
- Do you find yourself giving people unsolicited advice?
- Do you take responsibility for other people's duties? Are you the one always giving?
- Do you feel you need to be forceful to be heard or understood?
- How can you empower others to take responsibility for their own path?

Processing or Adopting Opinions of Others

When we worry about what others are doing, saying, thinking, and feeling, we drain ourselves of power. We step out of alignment with our Divine Self's wisdom and put our faith into the external environment. From this place, we are unable to make decisions for ourselves. We lose concentration because of our worry and doubt. We become stuck in the past and project our fears into the future. We cannot say no to others and are unable to confront situations with our full power.

Realize that everyone's opinions are situational and based on their own beliefs formed from their own experiences in life. Their beliefs and opinions have nothing to do with us and everything to do with them. Their interpretation of us is based on limited information and passed through the filter of their own belief system.

If we avoid confrontation because we do not want things to get worse, they probably will. If we are afraid of losing the relationship by acting and speaking authentically, we create our own prison. If others have opinions that aren't aligned with love and compassion, we can let their words pass by us. They are simply air and vibration. They cannot hurt us unless we give power to them to do so.

We are each incredibly valuable, and if a person leaves because of our honesty, we can release them and trust that more supportive friends and allies will come into our experience. Be honest about who you are and what you believe. Let it be seen. If we experience self-doubt, we can check to see if we have given away our power and formed an unhealthy dependency. We have the right to form our own opinions and believe in what is best for us.

- Are you afraid to behave or act in a certain way because of what people may think or do?
- Do you find yourself limiting yourself or holding back in any way because of what others may think, even fearing judgment from God? How does that affect you emotionally and physically?

Fear of Responsibility, Leadership, and True Empowerment

We can experience an imbalance in our Power Center if we have a fear of responsibility. We may believe that we are not able to be a leader and are afraid of taking charge. We may have judgments of power because we have seen people do harm with power and authority. We may associate wealth and power with greediness because we saw wealthy people and businesses take advantage of others. We may be afraid to stick out because of our role as a leader. We may fear power and leadership because we are afraid of failure.

Responsibility is the ability to follow our Inner Being's guidance and do what is best for us and the Greater Good of All. Accountability is the ability to take transparent ownership of our actions. What we decide to take on, we are accountable for. This means that we are ready to face situations without blaming others. These qualities give us the ability to lead and guide others on their path.

We have a responsibility to follow the desires of our souls to grow and expand through experience. When we hold ourself back from following our higher goals and aspirations, we may experience shame and guilt. When we are afraid of risk because we fear failure, we limit our growth and keep ourselves from experiencing the pleasure of success. If we desire to take action in the direction of our higher goals, we must take it or face the discomfort that comes from limiting our path.

- In what areas of your life do you procrastinate?
- Where can you show up more in your life?
- Where do you avoid people? Interactions? Places?

Discipline, Integrity, and Self-Respect

Integrity is a state of being whole and undivided by being honest and having strong moral principles and uprightness. When we are aligned with our Divine Self, we are whole and complete. When we align with our fears and doubt, we fracture ourselves into incomplete pieces.

When we act from a sense of morality and goodness, we harness our personal power. This is especially true when others are not aware of our actions or are present to witness them. Our Divine Self is always present, and when we act against our moral code or commit crimes, we shrink our personal power.

When we live a life of integrity and truth, we are prepared to express our authentic selves no matter what. We develop self-respect by living a life of righteousness and nobility. Living a noble life often means choosing courage over comfort and doing what is right versus doing what is popular, easy, and fast. When we live a noble life, we attract others who respect us because they see us as honorable.

- What gets in the way of accomplishing your goals in terms of fitness, finances, relationships, education, and spiritual growth?
- What practices and actions can you start today towards those goals?
- What support systems do you have in place to ensure that you are staying on your path? Do you have a mentor or an accountability partner?
- What rituals can you do to ensure positive momentum towards your goals and aspirations?

Solar Plexus Meditation

Close your eyes and begin to breathe consciously and deeply. If you would like, bring your hands to rest on your upper abdomen, your solar plexus. Imagine that within your solar plexus is your own personal sun. Using your breath and your imagination, make your sun grow brighter and stronger. Imagine and feel yourself as a divine, solar being. Feel your power and strength as a Divine Being of Light. If you feel any cords or attachments to your solar plexus, allow the light of your personal sun to burn them away. Feel your freedom. Feel your sovereignty.

Allow this Light and feeling to expand until it totally surrounds you. You can chant the sounds of RAM or OM to amplify this intention.

When you are finished, release the visualization. Open your eyes and continue your day with this feeling of empowerment and radiance.

SEVEN

Heart Chakra: Divine Love

T he Heart Chakra is located in the center of the chest and is associated with the color green, the wind element, and the breath of life. Universally, the heart is the symbol of our ability to love. The heart is where we express our devotion and connection to Source. The Heart Chakra bridges Spirit and the physical world, brings love-based spiritual insight to be used for heart-centered creation, and brings our human motivations up from the lower chakras to be transformed in the heart with spiritual wisdom. We broadcast this light out through our hearts to illuminate the world. Our heart sends waves of energy down through the arms and out through the hands to bless all that we touch. The heart is truly the gateway for ascension, the door to the Kingdom of Heaven. As we clear the heart of distortion, we see the Love of God shining back at us in all that we see.

The HeartMath Institute is a nonprofit organization that has researched and developed reliable, scientifically based tools to help people bridge the connection between their hearts and minds. Its research has discovered some impressive facts about the heart. When in utero, the heart develops before the brain and syncs with the heartbeat of our mother. The electromagnetic field of the heart, measuring five to eight feet away from our body, is the body's largest field and is constantly pulsing with information. More signals are sent from the heart to the brain than vice versa. The field of the heart has been measured to be 5,000 times stronger than the field of the brain.

Living "in the heart" gives you access to this powerful processing center. Living in the heart means processing our life events through the compassionate energy that is the heart center. When we focus on the pure energy at the core of our heart, we naturally emote loving-kindness, compassion, empathetic joy, equanimity, patience, and understanding.

When our Heart Center is balanced, we know that love is the most powerful force in the universe, and we see the goodness in people and the world. Our actions come from compassion, and we see and encourage goodness in others. When the Heart Chakra is balanced, we can accept the differences between ourselves and others easily. We live with a sense of unbridled joy and work to better the world around us. We are naturally generous and give from the heart without expectations. We use the heart to make decisions in our lives and receive intuitive information from our environment through the Unified Field. We understand the suffering of the world and are concerned with inequality and the harmful actions of others.

When this chakra is imbalanced, we may feel "hard-hearted" or "cold-hearted." We may build walls around our hearts to protect ourselves from getting hurt. We may see the world as a dark place, void of color and full of trickery and deceit. We may feel bitterness and be closed to the emotions of others and even be apathetic, unable to connect. We may judge ourselves and others by a harsh set of rules, regulations, and limitations. We may feel deeply hurt by others like a knife is lodged in our hearts. We may be ungiving, unloving, and grief-stricken. We may have a hard time forgiving ourselves or others and feel contempt and disdain for those who have wronged us.

When the heart is closed, we are closed to the unified field of Creation, so we are closed to our intuition and sense of the field we exist in. We may be dependent on others' love and attention because we have a gaping hole in our own love center. We may experience self-loathing and hold bitterness for others. The heart is truly where deep suffering is experienced.

We may experience health problems related to the heart and lungs. We may develop issues in the arms and hands. We may cave our chest, round the back, and feel armored and bound in the upper torso and neck. It could even be said that all illnesses and diseases stem from Heart Chakra imbalance because we have not been able to tune into the full redemptive powers of forgiveness, compassion, and unity.

What Imbalances the Heart Chakra?

Creating with the Heart vs. Creating with the Mind

The heart processes energy and emotional information. The heart can feel and sense into energy that is present and use it creatively for the greater good. It can feel into the past and into the future. It is intuitive in how it deciphers memory from the mind and information gained from the field. It leads to love and focuses on the positive of every situation. When we process experiences through the wisdom of the heart, we can never "get it wrong" because everything is processed from the perspective of growth and love.

The mind is the home of the egoic sense of "I" and "me," the limited self. The mind can create linearly. It can plan and strategize. It qualifies and values one experience over another. The mind, contaminated by the world's conditioned thought programs, distorts our reality through its biases and limited perspective.

If the mind is the realm where the battle between "good and evil" plays out, the heart is where we find true and lasting peace. The heart is the gateway to the Kingdom of Heaven. It is our access pathway to our Inner Being and the power that creates worlds. We can use our heart to process the energy of the mind so that we can move through life, making choices that align with our highest destiny pathway and the greater good of the All.

- Do you believe there is a right way or a wrong way to be or act?
- In what areas of your life do you hold polarized judgment?
- Where do you believe in good and bad, holy and sinful, safe and unsafe, worthy and unworthy? How do those beliefs feel in the body? How do they affect your mood and relationships with other people?

Expectations: Moving from the Heart to the Mind

When we have expectations of people and the world to be a certain way, we set ourselves up for disappointment. When we expect something, we move out of the heart's present awareness and into the duality of the mind and ego. The ego wants to control and possess reality. The mind wants to understand it. The heart has no expectations and loves what is.

Self-hatred and self-loathing develop when we place unreasonable expectations on ourselves and do not process life events with loving compassion. This may happen because we identify as our behaviors and actions, resulting in feeling guilt and regret. We are allowed to make mistakes and grow from them. When we punish ourselves from a perfectionist mindset, we close the heart and dampen our light.

The reconciliation process of the Ho'oponopono prayer "*I am sorry, I love you, please forgive me, I thank you.*" opens the heart to love and makes peace possible. You can say these phrases, sing them, write them, or even paint them. Use the process found in these words to reconcile your relationship with yourself, with another, with Source, with Gaia, or with anything or anyone else in your life that needs forgiveness.

We can forgive others even though they have not forgiven us. We can release the hurt. We can release the anger. If we genuinely want to be free from suffering, reconciliation and forgiveness are the way. If you forgive others and forgive yourself, half of the work is done, and peace is more possible for everyone involved. We do not have to condone the harmful actions of others, but we can forgive.

- What small things can you forgive today?
- Can you forgive someone who did something that caused you suffering that has a medium charge?
- Can you forgive someone who did a terrible thing to you?
- Can you forgive people who have done the worst things to the planet, animal life, and humanity? Where can you do your part in healing resentment?

Egoic Love versus Universal Unconditional Love

Unconditional Love is the animating force and foundation of the universe. The Source of Love is always flowing to us, and there is nothing we can do to stop this outpouring of Love and Grace. We can, however, block this love from coming into our experience. When the heart is closed, we inhibit the flow of Universal Love that wants to express itself through us.

The ego can create an idea of love that is based on possession and control. Much of what mainstream culture considers to be love has truly little to do with the heart chakra. It focuses on the concept of love created by the personality. This type of love is generated in the lower chakras and is not the same as the Divine Love found within the heart.

When we are in egoic love, we see love as a sense of ownership and contractual agreement. Egoic love uses the attention, presence, and affection of another person to fulfill sensory desires. Egoic love has rules and regulations for how love and affection can be expressed. Ego says that we can only love one person, and they are required to fulfill us on all levels.

When we love without conditions, we set our relations free to follow their own path. We allow them to be and explore as they wish. Loving a person does not mean we control them. Being loved does not mean we are being controlled. All are free to follow their highest joy from moment to moment. We accept them as they are and take responsibility for our own joy and well-being.

Egoic trust is a concept based on control and manipulation. Egoic love says, "I trust you to do what I want to satisfy my needs." while Universal Love says, "I release you to do what you need to support yourself. I love you as you are." True trust is placing our faith in Source and knowing that all is happening as it should and that we are eternally provided for.

Everyone is behaving in a way that reflects their own beliefs and attitudes towards life. Another person's hurtful actions reflect their own mindset and have nothing to do with us. We can look at someone's behavior and intuitively know what actions to take. Maybe that means not being around them. Maybe that means using our voice to communicate that we are experiencing hurt. We can make adjustments in our relationships without any love being lost.

- When do you withhold affection towards others?
- When do you close your heart to others?
- When do you feel hurt by others?
- When do you want to punish others?
- When do you feel your judgments and rage are justified?

Blind Love and Blind Faith

Blind love and blind faith happen when our expression and experience of love are based on illusion and fantasy. This happens when we run with our emotions, sensations, and fantasies and do not see ourselves and the other in truth. This type of love is full of dependency and impulses to maintain the illusion and naive story we tell ourselves. When we live like this, we ignore what is right in front of our noses and make a habit of overlooking or denying the reality of other people's hurtful actions and behaviors.

True love is willing to look at deeper truth and accept the deeper meanings of what we find. We can love and keep boundaries. We can love and keep our intelligence, clarity, and groundedness.

- Are there people in your life that are behaving in a way that does not honor you?

- Are there any relationships where you can be more honest with yourself about certain dynamics or red flags?
- What spells do you cast on yourself to habitually overlook these issues?

Feelings of Betrayal: A Broken Heart

Everyone is always following what they feel is best for them from moment to moment. They are doing their best, even if they may be guided by selfishness, greed, anger, or fear. They are doing what they think is best, and it has little to do with "you." In this way, there is no such thing as a betrayal. People are following their Inner Being and mind.

If you feel as though someone has taken something from you or betrayed you in any way, they have given you something much more valuable. They teach you where your dependencies are. They teach you where you are conditional with love. They teach you where you have put your faith in something outside of yourself to bring you joy and completion. We can take full responsibility for our emotions and mental health and understand that everything is happening for a higher purpose. Everyone is free to do what they need to do to allow joy and love into their lives. When everyone is free to choose, love abounds. This does not mean that you condone negative behavior or spiritually bypass it, but you can come to a deeper understanding of the cause of your suffering.

- Where do you blame others for your suffering?
- Do you believe someone or some group has betrayed you or your family?
- Can you grow in compassion and a higher understanding of the nature of your suffering?

Honor Thy Body as Thy Temple

Self-soothing and self-care honor the union of the body, mind, and spirit. Dedicate your life to learning to love yourself more. When you love yourself, you experience love with others easily. Take long baths. Go into nature. Dress yourself up. Sing to yourself. Marry your essence and promise to cherish it forever and ever. Fall endlessly in love with the light that you are.

- Do you take enough "time off" and have enough alone time?

- Do you treat yourself to luxuries or gifts from time to time? Do you feel guilty or feel you need to justify this?
- How can you treat your body better?
- How can you treat your heart better?

Desires of the Bodymind

We have many layers of desire, manifesting, and evolving. We have desires of the body to walk, run, and eat. We have desires of the mind to grow, learn, and plan. Our senses desire to touch, taste, smell, hear, and experience. All are temporary experiences and beautiful.

True and lasting nourishment comes from spiritual growth and our alignment with the Love of the Universe. When we tend to the desire of the heart and soul to evolve and expand with love, we are filled with the deepest sense of satisfaction and wholeness. When we follow the desires of the senses, we follow the maya, the illusion.

The heart desires recognition. It desires purification. It desires to love with no bounds. When we do the work to dissolve our limiting beliefs and heal from our past traumas, we allow the Love of the Universe to flow through us, as us, and we embody the Light of the Divine.

- Where are your addictions? How do they affect your life?
- What needs are you not taking care of?
- Do you have a strong and consistent spiritual practice?
- How can you expand or deepen it?

Creating Coherence in Your Life

"Coherence is the state when the heart, mind, and emotions are in energetic alignment and cooperation," HeartMath Institute Research Director Dr. Rollin McCraty says. "It is a state that builds resiliency — personal energy is accumulated, not wasted — leaving more energy to manifest intentions and harmonious outcomes."

Personal Coherence

When we are coherent, our heart and mind work together to find optimal experiences and creative solutions. We are living in connection with the wisdom of our inner Source and have more intuitive access and flow. We can tap into our inner technology and multidimensional being to uplevel communication with the world around us. This slows down the mind and opens our higher perceptual centers of the brain (cortical facilitation). It is said "a change of the heart changes everything," for when we live through the heart's wisdom, we are open to experiences beyond our current cognitive understanding.

Social Coherence

When we are in a state of personal coherence, everything and everyone around us benefits. We raise the vibrational frequency of the field around us and create the potential for higher outcomes for all. Our mere presence is a blessing and a catalyst for healing and spiritual growth. This can also inspire others to drop into their own state of personal coherence.

When this happens, we sync up energetically, connected heart to heart, and communicate on unseen levels. We feel each other on a deep level and hold each other in the best light.

Global Coherence

When we are in a state of personal coherence, we are connected to universal and planetary energies. We stand as a bridge between physical and nonphysical reality and feel a deep connection to All That Is. When we are in a state of coherence, we are connected to the Earth's holographic field and the collective mind of humanity. Like a moving, living prayer, we are broadcasting an invitation for global peace and unity. When we take the time to anchor ourselves in loving awareness, we create the potential for Heaven on Earth. On the New Earth, all of humanity will be united in global coherence.

Coherence Meditation: Inspired by HeartMath Institute

Close your eyes and begin to breathe deep and satisfying breaths. Feel the length of your spine and allow your shoulders to fall away from the ears. Deepen and elongate the breath and completely focus on the act of breathing for a few moments. Bring your hands to rest on your heart center and imagine that you can breathe in and out of your heart center. Imagine that in the center of your heart is a spark of divine white light. As you breathe in and out, allow that light to grow and shine brighter. Allow this light to extend beyond your body until it totally surrounds you with beautiful white light. Make it sparkle and shine. Imagine that you can breathe this Light into your being and allow it to fill your entire body.

Think of something that brings you joy. Maybe it is a loved one. Maybe it is a sunny day. Bring into your mind images, sensations, and feelings connected to this object or experience that brings you joy. Continue to breathe in and out as you imagine all of the blessings and appreciations of your life. Feel this joy spreading throughout your entire field.

You can chant the sounds of YAM, OM, HU, or AH to amplify these vibrations.

Stay with this feeling for a few moments. Then, be silent and listen to your Inner Being and return to normal breathing. When you are finished, open your eyes feeling deeply blessed by this experience.

EIGHT

Throat Chakra:
Conscious Communication

Our Throat Center radiates out from the center of our vocal instrument and is associated with the color blue and with the element of ether. It governs our ability to communicate, and I also associate this chakra with vibration and sound.

We use our voice to share our thoughts, desires, and intentions with the world. This center also gives us the ability to hear and sense what is being communicated by others. The power of the word has the potential to create or destroy. When we speak from our fear or pain, our words are like poison that can rob us and others of life force. Our words can create walls of separation that keep us from having relationships built on love and trust.

When we align our voice and communication with our divine nature, we cultivate intimate connections based on transparency and honesty. We can listen to the deeper meaning of what is being communicated by others. When we communicate from a pure center, we can turn mishaps into miracles and speak our dreams into creation.

We communicate to change our environment and modify our relationships. We use language and communication to interact with others, exchange ideas, and express ourselves. When we cannot communicate clearly, we miss out on opportunities and confuse ourselves and others.

When our Throat Center is balanced, we communicate our thoughts, desires, and intentions clearly. We are articulate and deliberate with our use of language and expression, using our voice as a powerful tool for manifestation. We are persuasive and charismatic and easily manifest our ideas into reality. We comfortably speak in front of groups and may actually enjoy the act of speaking publicly. We are succinct and compassionate with our words and value the honesty and straightforwardness of others. We can hear the deeper truth in what is being communicated by others and speak directly to the soul of another person. We value quietness and use our awareness to listen to the communication of our Inner Being.

When our Throat Center is imbalanced, we may easily follow other people's will because we cannot communicate our own desires and vision. We may have trouble finding the right words to express our own perspective. We may lie, tell partial truths, exaggerate the truth, and play with words to get what we want. We may say what we think others want to hear. We may feel like something is blocked in our throats as we suppress our voice out of fear and self-doubt. We may drop our own plans at the first perceived sign of conflict and opposition. We may speak harshly and use nasty words that are bitter and riddled with resentment.

If the energy of our throat center is overactive, we may try extra hard to convince others. We may be overly talkative with the belief that no one is listening. We may cut people off, talk over them, or interrupt other people's sentences. We may hold our breath in our chest, waiting for the moment to jump in, unable to deeply listen to what others are communicating. If the throat center is underactive, we may have an underlying belief that it is best if we are silent and act timid or shy. We may withhold information out of fear of what people may think or do. We may say things we do not really mean and feel guilty later.

Imbalances of the throat chakra can manifest as throat, ear, and thyroid issues. Often people will start to lose their hearing because they need to listen to their Inner Being more attentively. Those with hyperactive thyroids most likely have subconscious beliefs that propel them to be overactive talkers while hypoactive means someone's belief system is keeping them from speaking their truth or else tells them that they should be quiet.

What Imbalances the Throat Chakra?

Imbalances in the Throat Center have roots in the first four chakras because we need to feel safe, connected to our inherent value, empowered, and connected to our heart's deepest truth to communicate honestly and transparently. We may be afraid of damaging or losing relationships. We may be afraid of sounding harsh and filter what we are communicating. We may feel and fear that others may think we are unintelligent. We may fear being wrong and remain silent. We may be afraid of causing conflict or debate. Maybe we are uncertain what could happen if we express ourselves fully and authentically. If we feel inferior or even superior to others, we may adapt our communication and expression to match that belief. We could fear being abandoned, shamed, ridiculed, or rejected for communicating or expressing authentically. We may fear to express ourselves on any level simply because we are afraid of being vulnerable.

This is a massive wound for the human collective as we emerge from the Dark Ages. Females and the Divine Feminine have been repressed and oppressed for thousands of years. Many of us carry lifetimes of trauma related to our throat center. A big part of our awakening is healing the wounds of the past and finding our voice. We also have a responsibility to use our voice for the voiceless, including the women, children, Indigenous peoples, Gaia, animals, trees, and others who have been silenced and oppressed.

What Balances the Throat Center?

Take Responsibility for Your Reality

Everything is happening because on some level, consciously or unconsciously, we have willed it into being. Our fears, thoughts, actions, intentions, and vibrational offerings create our reality. No one else is to blame for our experience of reality. When we take authority over our experience, we use our voice to create the life we want.

Every time we say the words "I will" and "I am," the following words have an effect on the body and mind. These are spells we put on ourselves. Be very deliberate and care-FULL of how you use your words.

- What thoughts and communication patterns cause you suffering?
- Do you speak in ways that belittle or disempower yourself or others?
- Do you speak in a way that paints a negative picture or victim perspective of your life or future?

Honesty and Integrity: Tell the Truth

Telling mistruths and lies blocks our Throat Center. It depletes us of life force energy immediately. This lowers our vibration and changes our point of attraction. Instead of saying mistruth, we can say, "I don't know," when we do not. Instead of speaking on someone else's behalf, we can say, "This is not my place. It is better to ask them." Gossip and character assassination hurt us way before it hurts another.

- Where do you tell white lies?
- Do you exaggerate or withhold information out of fear of what the outcome might be or out of fear of judgment?
- Where do you speak on behalf of others?

Be Impeccable With & Honor Your Words

When we say we are going to do something, we should be sure that we can follow through. When we honor our words, our yes means "yes," and our no means "no." If we are uncertain, we can communicate that we need more time or that we are not certain that we can commit at this time. We can feel into our body and sense our Inner Being to feel our truth. If something is even a little wobbly, honor that. If we make a decision, we are allowed to change our mind. Communicate it as soon as you are aware of the change.

- Do you follow your own agreements?
- How likely are you to follow through with verbal agreements?
- How do you notify people when you become aware of changes?
- Do you have any hesitation? How does it feel in the body?

Lost in Translation

Try your best to communicate important matters face to face, or at the very least make a phone call. Too often, important matters are discussed via text or social media. So much is lost in translation. Most of what is communicated is nonverbal anyway. We are empathetic and observant beings. We need body language, energy, and the presence of the other beings we are communicating with to experience all that is being expressed and communicated fully.

- Have you called the people you love lately?
- Are there any communications that you should address more personally rather than through text or email?

Check connections to Solar Plexus, Sacral, and Root Center beliefs to clarify the Throat Center distortions.

Release Guilt

Guilt happens when we have not met our own expectations. If we do not settle our guilt, the situation, circumstances, or feeling comes around repeatedly. We can get caught in a cycle of behavior-guilt-justification, behavior-guilt-justification, etc.

Our guilt is there as a teacher. It shows us where we are off in our beliefs and helps us to adjust our behavior to achieve optimal and pleasurable experiences. We can realize that the guilt is self-created, strive to understand its origins, release it, and find a solution that reflects expanded awareness.

A lot of religions teach that God judges and punishes us based on our actions. Source/God/All-That-Is loves you completely and wants your success and liberation. There is infinite grace for all our stumbles. Guilt is the creation of the ego. Each ego has a different definition of what behaviors are unworthy or punishable. These are all illusions. Divine Love and Grace are available at all times for ALL people, regardless of past behavior. Release guilt and allow your voice to express freely.

- Where can you forgive yourself for past deeds?
- What lifestyle and ethical changes can you implement today to create a more authentic life?

Release Jealousy & Realize Equality

We experience jealousy when comparing a limited aspect of someone else with limited aspects of ourselves. Experiencing ourselves as inferior or superior in comparison creates division and separation. Everyone and everything are equal. Everyone has a unique purpose and unique expression to accomplish within the continuum of evolution.

- What criteria have you used to evaluate who is above and who is below you?
- Do you think you are better than others? Inferior?
- Do you envy what others have?
- Do you compare yourself to others?

Release Beliefs of Dependency

When we feel that we are dependent on others or that others are dependent on us, we can say what we think they want to hear or use our words to manipulate them. When we have healthy interdependence in our relationships, each person honors and values the other's honesty, transparency, and vulnerability. When we release beliefs of unhealthy dependency, everyone is responsible for their own well-being and experience.

- Where are you afraid to take action or assert boundaries because of beliefs of dependency?

Notice Argument Patterns

"Never argue with a fool." —Albert Einstein

As people argue, they get more and more specific about what they do not like, which creates a stronger and stronger negative charge, attracting more instability and hostility. We have become a culture of "debate" versus a society of mature, transparent dialogue. The ego says these are "my" beliefs and has a hard time accepting differences. The Self can hold perspective and be open to seeing from another's perspective without fear of the loss of power or identity.

When a conversation gets heated, go general and light. If the person you are communicating with wants to get deeper and deeper into the details and suffering and you follow along, a professional arguer who is unmovable in their perception and intention to dominate will eventually wear you down to their emotional and vibrational level and overpower you. You know what is true in your heart. Speak your truth simply, then let it go. You are not responsible for changing someone's mind. They are. Walk away and find something better to do.

- Do you have people that you regularly argue with?
- Do you expect people should see things how you do because your way is right or better?
- How open are you to changing your own perceptions and beliefs when presented with new data? Is there room for all perspectives and opinions?

- Do you try to "win" in conversations? If so, the relationship loses.
- What happens to your physical body when you argue?

Heart-Centered Communication: Identifying with Your Soul

Speak from your loving heart. If you cannot speak from a loving place, it is best to find another time to communicate and express what is rising within you. Identifying with your suffering — "I am angry." versus "I am the awareness that experiences anger." are two very different perspectives. Spend some quiet time in reflection and self-soothing to raise your vibration. Spend time with your Inner Being to find the message from your Higher Self.

Illusion of Good & Bad

Good and bad are judgments and definitions made up by the dualistic nature of the human ego. Each person has their own definition of good and bad. Judging something or someone as bad lowers our vibration and causes us to suffer.

When we look at our experiences and relationships with compassion, when we look deeply into the cause of the behavior or experience, we can find compassion and a higher spiritual meaning. Everything simply IS, but we place meaning and judgments on Creation. When we accept things as they are and release our definitions, we can see the bigger picture.

- Where do you project meaning onto events and people?

Frustration: Things Left Unsaid

When you are in a state of frustration, your intelligence stops working. Stop. Take a breath. If you are frustrated and others are involved, remember that you are frustrated with the experience and not the souls of the beings involved. People are not their behaviors. Learn to work with their shortcomings. Set a boundary if necessary.

- What are some healthy ways to deal with conflict to keep your cool so you can speak from your center?
- What is the core cause of your frustration? Check your dependencies.

The Magic of Words

Words can be like white magic or black magic. They can be in Service to the Greater Good or service to our ego. As we become more and more deliberate with our words, intonation, and delivery, we begin to become powerful masters of manifestation.

Using our words for dark magic happens when we use words with the vibration of fear and judgment. Using our words for white magic means that we use our words to intentionally elevate our experience with love. Realize that it is not WHAT you speak but HOW you communicate that matters. Are you speaking from fear and suffering? Are you speaking from love and compassion? Coming from love means that there is love within you and that you create from that compassionate perspective. This type of love is not superficial. It is unconditional and regenerative.

- How can you use your words, spoken internally and externally, to create more of what you want?
- When do you use your words to give power to the shadow creation?

Throat Chakra Meditation

Close your eyes and begin to breathe consciously and deeply for a few breaths. Bring your hands to lightly touch or hold them slightly away from your throat while you tune into the subtle vibrations of the hands and Throat Center. Imagine that the center of your throat has a beautiful, dazzling flame of blue-white light. Softly begin to make long tones. Make them feel soothing and imagine that the sounds are originating from your Inner Being. You may use a sound like HAM, OM, or any other sound that feels good for you. If any judgmental thoughts arise, let them dissolve into the healing tones and bring your awareness back to your Inner Being.

Allow yourself to be playful and create your own angelic tones, your own language of Light.

Connect with a sense of beauty and orchestrate a tonal symphony with many ranges of tones. Let the tones move throughout your body. Send the healing vibrations into all of your tissues and cells. Imagine that each cell begins to reverberate with these healing tones. Fill your body with light and vibration. Do this for at least a minute or two.

Once you are complete, return to silence, and feel the vibrations and sensations in your throat center. When you are finished, open your eyes.

NINE

Brow Chakra: Divine Vision

The Brow Center, located within the forehead and associated with the color indigo, gives us spiritual sight and the ability to perceive our inner and outer world. This inner eye gives us the ability to see beyond physicality and perceive through foresight and intuition. There are differing elemental associations with this chakra, but I connect it to Light.

Often called the "third eye," this center senses the blueprint and matrix of the Unified Field and what is needed to manifest an idea into reality. Like an internal movie screen, the Brow Center allows us to receive internal imagery from other people, our Higher Self, guides, and Source. It allows us to project imagery and thoughtforms into the matrix to draw forth our manifested desires and outcomes like a broadcasting device and homing beacon. It connects us to the essence of life, giving us the ability to make clear decisions that resonate with the Light of our Inner Being. Physical manifestations of dysfunction in the Brow Center include issues with the eyes and brain.

When this center is balanced, we can quickly see the inner workings of things and what is needed to maintain balance and harmonic evolution. We enjoy the challenge of finding creative solutions and can lead with a clear vision, mental focus, and intuition. We are able to create goals and envision the pathway to successfully achieving them. We can ride the waves of life with ease and make quick decisions sourced from profound understanding and insight. We can understand the deeper intention of people's motives through a telepathic connection and exchange. We can self-reflect and receive guidance from psychic perceptions. We can understand complex issues while also having the openness to see life from a different perspective.

When this center is imbalanced, we are easily confused and have trouble focusing and grounding. Our uncertainty and lack of consistent and clear focus on our vision create issues with manifesting what we truly wish to cultivate. Decision-making is slow because we overthink the possibilities. We may force our ideas and perceptions on others because we cannot think beyond our current paradigm. We may be stubborn, skeptical, and have unwavering tunnel vision regarding our beliefs. We may resent others for their achievements because we cannot see our own potential or feel blocked when turning our dreams into reality. We may be skeptical of new systems and new concepts because we do not understand them and cannot think outside our own paradigm. We may avoid the reality of our life circumstances, seeing only what we want to see.

Health problems associated with this energy center include all cognitive and brain health-related issues such as memory loss and difficulty with concentration and also include issues with the eyes, ears, and nose.

What Imbalances the Brow Chakra?

Confusion: Trouble Making Decisions

This center becomes imbalanced when we are afraid of making the wrong decisions or afraid of a future failure. This creates a struggle in our mind as we bounce back and forth between potential outcomes and risks. When we are in alignment, we make decisions that honor our Inner Being and our environment. We make decisions based on our NOW moment. What feels good now? What honors my soul now? Be careful with this as the ego/mind often masquerades as enlightened consciousness and many avoid spiritual growth by creating comfort for the mind. When we take care of our own energy and Inner Being first, everything else falls into place.

- When making a decision, do you feel pressure to make "the right decision?"
- What concerns do you habitually have when making day-to-day decisions and bigger decisions when more is at stake?
- How do you respond to inner imagery, inner guidance, and intuition?
- Do you follow your guidance or doubt and suppress it?

Living in the Past

We are only supposed to know the past happened. We are not supposed to live there. Our awareness of our past experiences gives us an idea of what we enjoy and what we do not enjoy. Our future is made of our choices and our vibration of the present moment. So often, people project their fears and traumas from the past into their vision of the future. When you hold a vision and vibration of what you do not want, you create it. To manifest what we truly desire, we can hold an inspired vision and emotional vibration that matches our desired outcome.

To make a decision, connect with your Inner Being and your Inner Light, then ask your body, mind, and senses what decision is best for you NOW. Asking others blocks your own intelligence and may confuse you even more. What decision inspires YOU? What decision honors YOUR Inner Being and Divine Self?

- Do you project fearful outcomes into your future when planning and making decisions? If so, what happened in your past that makes you feel that way?
- What is your general outlook on the future?

Physical & Mental Attachments

Clinging to or grasping at people, places, things, and ideas keeps us from seeing the bigger picture. We may begin to believe that we NEED something and that our happiness would be lost without our object of desire. Attachments cause suffering and limit our ability to see the bigger picture.

Shedding attachments does not mean neglecting ourselves or keeping ourselves from having experiences that we enjoy. It does not mean we should leave our beloved, sell our house, or not have nice things. It is, however, inaccurate to believe that our happiness comes from having those things. Our partner may decide to leave, or our house may burn down, and now the same object that once was associated with joy is associated with suffering. We easily allow joy to move through us when our manifestations match our desires. Even in the absence of them, we can still allow joy into our experience. Everything outside of ourselves just simply exists, and we project meaning onto it. When we release our attachments, we can experience life in pure loving awareness without the need to cling to any circumstance or manifestation to experience joy and wholeness.

- Where are your attachments? What outside of yourself do you give power to?
- How do you behave when you feel attached and dependent?

Desires & Aversions

Strong feelings of distaste, resentment, and resistance inhibit our perception of the divine perfection in all things. When we have deep-seated hatred or detestation, we lower our vibration and poison our own self. If we condemn something outside of ourselves, we are the ones who experience the suffering connected to the judgment. When we learn to release judgment and the resistance it generates, we can see life without the lens of duality.

- Where are your aversions? Where do you have automatic responses of rejection and denial?

Egoic Identity Structure

The ego, the personality, is our sense of "me" or "I." The ego is not our True Nature because it changes and evolves. Sometimes it is present and sometimes it is not such as in deep sleep. It is a projection of the mind that veils our True Nature.

Ego identification creates an illusion that we are separate from others. It takes limited pieces of information and creates definitions and judgments based on that limited information. The ego filters our present and future through past experiences and trauma. When we release our ego's definitions and positions, we can perceive the world clearly. To perceive clearly, it is essential that we connect with the power of our Inner Being that sees beyond concept, duality, definition, and judgment.

- Where do you have attachments and emotional investments in the belief of a separate self?
- What instinctual drives do you act upon that do not serve your highest and best growth?

Ignorance

Ignorance, misconceptions, misunderstandings, and incorrect knowledge block people from making clear decisions that support their highest development. To be born on Earth is to be born into ignorance. Our body could not sustain the full brilliance of our True Nature; it would burn out!

It is okay to be uneducated and ignorant about things. You can always learn more. Education empowers the individual to make better decisions. We can strive to dissolve our ignorance by actively learning and growing. We can read, study, and become wiser on any subject and choose an informed position.

- Are there topics or areas of life that you feel drawn to learn more about?
- How often do you read sacred texts?
- What practices of self-study do you implement regularly?
- How do you expand your internal library?

Will to Live: Fear of Death and Change

The desire to keep living and the fear of change are buried deep within our subconscious. The fear of death can keep us from seeing life clearly and from doing things that we may truly enjoy. If we cling to physical life, we cling to impermanence and we inherently suffer. We may subconsciously protect ourselves and "keep it safe" to avoid the real or imagined danger that keeps us from the spiritual growth available in new situations. We can develop trust in the support of the Divine and rest in knowing that we are always guided.

- What are your beliefs around death and what happens to you when you die?
- Do you have any fears of what the repercussions of your death may bring?
- How do you deal with the death of other people or the truth that we all go through the death experience?

Brow Center Meditation

Close your eyes and breathe consciously and deeply. You can bring one hand to the front of your brow and one hand to the back of your skull, cupping the bony ridge of the occiput. Sense the space between your hands. Imagine a spark of light within your brow center that grows bigger and brighter as you breathe in and out. If your mind is busy, imagine that your thoughts are like clouds in the sky and allow them to drift by until you see only a beautiful, clear blue sky.

Take a few moments to envision yourself as clear and confident. Allow your mind to generate images, feelings, and sensations of what it would be like if everything you desire to create was already here. Where would you live? What kind of activities would you be involved in? How would your relationships look if everything were ideal? What would you create with your time? What would the world look like? How would it feel to be your ideal future self? How would you move in the world? Have fun envisioning the images and evoking the feelings of your ideal future reality.

Envision your neural pathways weaving new circuitry to prepare to "dock" with that future reality. Feel your cells beginning to light up, transform, and prepare to experience this ideal reality. Feel the universe restructuring to bring you all that you desire. Feel your deservedness of perfection in all ways. Charge yourself up with pure creative potential.

When you are finished, you can chant the sounds of OM to amplify these healing intentions. When you are finished, drop the visualization, return to normal breathing, and open your eyes.

TEN

Crown Chakra: Divine Limitlessness

The Crown Center, blooming from the crown of the head, is the entryway of universal consciousness into our physical body. Different traditions have different elemental associations. I think of it as the unity of all elements, sounds, and vibrations or the pure thoughtform transmission of the divine energy.

This chakra is called the "thousand-petaled lotus" and is associated with brilliant white or radiant violet. It is our connection to the greater Universal Hologram of Unity and Oneness. We use this center when we are in experiences of wonder and connection to All That Is such as when we walk through the magic of a forest or look at a beautiful sunset. As we open this center, we allow the Light of the Divine to fill our being with grace and openness.

Through this center, we trust in Divine Timing and our higher understanding and know that all is in Divine Perfection. We know that everything is happening for the greater good. It is our connection to our battery (Source) and the limitless energy of the Divine. This center is activated through acts of service and devotion. We see the image of the Crown Chakra around paintings of Jesus, the Holy Mother, Quan Yin, and Buddha to show the power of their enlightenment made possible through their Crown Center. Physical dysfunction of Crown Chakra imbalances involves issues with the brain.

When the Crown Center is balanced, we may feel like we are wearing a shining crown of Light. We radiate presence and patience and are in collaboration with Divine Timing. We experience synchronicities and feel connected to the magic and miracles of Life. We are deeply satisfied as we are nourished through our connection to All That Is, and we ARE that! We are connected to our soul purpose and have deliberate intent in our interactions with Life. We see mishaps and mistakes as learning opportunities and use them to grow consciously. We easily guide and support others because we are tapped into our Divine Essence. We experience bliss, gratitude, and a deep connection with Life and take personal responsibility for our alignment. We experience the miraculous unfolding of life seen through direct perception, openness, and bliss.

When this center is imbalanced, we are disconnected from our battery and divine guidance. We may place our faith in external authority figures, government systems, and religious figures. We may be easily discouraged and feel spiritually disconnected, blaming our misfortunes on destiny, genetics, our culture, ethnicity, luck, God, or the universe. This can cause depression, hopelessness, worthlessness, and despair. We may feel that life is meaningless and without purpose. We may be critical of other people's beliefs about politics and world affairs. This is the center of religious fanaticism, grandeur, and the God/Messiah complex. We may desire spiritual dominance over others, even to the point of being worshipped by them. The opposite is also true. We may deny spiritual reality or be critical of others' spiritual practices and beliefs.

What Imbalances the Crown Center?

Dissatisfaction

In each moment, we are currently receiving everything that we are a vibrational match to. We do not get more for being a "good person." We do not receive less for being a "bad person." Look at society, and you will see this is true. If we desire more and it is not manifesting, we can grow and change. The universe is energy and vibration. We can raise our vibration and become a match to our desires.

When we hold the energy of dissatisfaction, we hold the vibration of lack of manifested desire, and what we want cannot come to us. We are blocking our own desires from manifesting. We can find gratitude for what we have and do the work to grow spiritually to achieve our higher aspirations.

- Where can you grow in appreciation for yourself and the blessings of your life?
- In what areas of your life do you experience dissatisfaction?

Perceived Limitations

The Crown Center connects us to our infinite potential. It is our connection to the Oneness, and it connects us to the truth of our limitlessness.

Our beliefs of limitation, whether self-created or indoctrinated from the world, keep us from experiencing the fullness of who and what we are. If we have beliefs of limitation, we will experience them. We can release our beliefs of limitation and allow our intelligence to guide us through each moment of discovery and expansion.

When we project our beliefs of limitation onto others, we cannot see them in their full potential. We see them in limitation. When we empower others to be more, do more, and follow their own guidance, we watch them blossom into their fullness. This is true love.

To reach our full potential, we can dream bigger and allow our imagination to dream up a new reality and paradigm. We are here to develop spiritualized consciousness. We are here to push the edges of what we think is real. We are pioneers on the leading edge of consciousness with the blessed gift of this life to pioneer new frontiers of perception and embodiment.

- Where do you believe you are limited?

Fear of Death

Fear of any kind immediately distorts our crown and root chakras, cutting us off from our connection to the Earth and our connection to Source. When we leave this body, we live on in other forms. Most of what we are is outside of this body. We are eternal beings. When we fear death, we keep ourselves from receiving all the wonderful energy of the universe that wants to flow through us. To truly live, we need to make peace with the fact that we will leave this body one day.

This is apparent when observing who in the population is stepping into sovereignty and ascension and who is hiding away in fear and buying the media and government narratives. Fear closes the Crown chakra and keeps people from receiving the higher evolutionary coding. Truly, these next few years will "separate the wheat from the chaff" as we are presented with opportunities to reconcile all fear and come into Trust and Unity with our True Nature.

- Have you made peace with the idea that you will experience physical death?
- Have you made peace with the idea that those you love will experience physical death?

The Illusion of Luck

Luck is a superstitious belief that blocks us from our full potential as masterful creators. Believing in luck places our power outside of ourselves. We are always manifesting what matches our vibration or what is best for our path. If we feel that we have bad luck, we can practice self-inquiry to understand what limiting beliefs or energies we hold to manifest the "bad luck."

- Where do you believe in luck or superstition? Where do you place power outside of your own divine ability to manifest?

Traumatic Experiences

Emotional and physical trauma can keep us locked in our past experiences. It can keep us focused on the transient parts of our smaller self (i.e., mind, emotions, body) so that we lose awareness of our Divine Self. We could think, "Why me?" or even blame God, "Why have you forsaken me?" Healing our trauma allows us to open to our Higher Self and our limitlessness.

- Do you blame God for anything? Do you feel cursed or limited by your past actions?

Distorted Ideas about Money, Wealth, and Power

We are powerful beings of Creation. To embody that potential, we can investigate our ideas about wealth, money, and power. We are currently getting everything we deserve, and we are worth SO MUCH MORE. The universe is abundant in nature. There is plenty to go around, and there is always more. Maybe we learned that we don't deserve richness or have accepted that people with money are bad. Maybe we hoard our money out of fear that there won't be any tomorrow. When we hold the vibration of lack, that is what we create.

Money is an energy exchange that likes to flow. When we need to pay money, we can allow it to leave our possession graciously, knowing that more is always coming. When someone offers us a gift from the heart of any kind, we can receive it with gratitude. This sends a message out to the universe that we are open to receiving. This also allows the circuit of goodwill and abundance to continue flowing throughout the world. If you have a habit of evading gifts or blessings from others, notice how it feels in your body the next time an opportunity to receive arises.

- What are your beliefs about money, wealth, and power?
- How does that get outpictured in your life or keep you from taking steps that would benefit your relationships, career, and finances?

Denial of the Divine

To complete our ascension, it is essential to open to the Living Light of God, the Limitless Light of Source accessed through our own reaching towards Higher Love. This often means that we move beyond our mental constructs of the Godhead and learn to have an experiential relationship with the Divine through our crown and heart chakras. The Living God is beyond all religious concepts and beyond the duality of human consciousness. We must invite the presence of the Divine, the Holy Spirit, to make a home within us. We cannot make the quantum leap of Ascension without that relationship and harmonic connection.

The Divine Presence is always there; our True Nature always exists. When we are in our joy, the Light of Awareness is there with us. When we are doing something out of integrity, the Light of Awareness is still there as we act it out and follow the mind or the impulses of the body. It is up to each of us to commit to moment-to-moment living to perceive that unwavering, ever-present, changeless presence that pervades All!

This is especially true in these times as people have a limited perspective and understanding of what the Divine Plan is. Everything is Source. Everything is God. Nothing can ever be separate from it. When we judge something as wrong or evil, we deny the presence of the Divine within the manifestation and follow the duality. All is Source Consciousness projecting a transactional reality in evolution. As we learn to step out of the shrunken, distorted perceptions of duality, we can learn to live in fascination and awe of the many faces of the Divine. Even the battle between "good and evil" arises, abides, and dissolves within the pure brilliance of Source.

This does not mean that we should not try to improve the quality of life upon the planet or that we should spiritually bypass the suffering of others.

It means that we can face the challenges of life with this higher understanding and use our spiritual understanding to guide the world into greater states of harmony and balance.

- Is there anything that you judge as outside of or separate from God? If so, where does that belief come from?

Crown Chakra Meditation

Close your eyes and breathe consciously and deeply. Bring your attention to the crown of your head and imagine that it is opening up like a thousand-petaled lotus flower. Imagine that each petal is shining with pure white light with rainbow sparkles. Use your hands to "fluff up" the emanations of the Crown Chakra. Make it shine and make it beautiful. Imagine that universal energy is flowing into this luminous lotus, filling it with cosmic knowledge of the Divine. See this radiant energy flowing into the crown of your head. You can chant the sound of OM repeatedly and feel the vibration of this mantra radiating from the crown of your head. Give gratitude for the opportunity to awaken and unite with the Divine.

Play with this visualization for a few minutes. When you are finished, return to normal breathing, and feel the vibrations you have generated. Open your eyes and enjoy the rest of your day!

ELEVEN

Ascension Chakras

Described below are some of the less commonly known chakras that are now resurfacing in human awareness. Each of them gives access to unique energies and sources of information. I have included a basic practice for each chakra to help you connect with it. In the back of the book, I have written an entire manual to guide you through the art of laying hands. Included in the "Laying Hands: Reiki and Beyond" section, you will find instructions on how to heal yourself and assist others in healing by learning to channel Source Light. There are also instructions on hand and body mudras to help your body channel and transmit spiritual light. Be sure to check it out!

Soul Star Chakra

Located approximately six inches above the head is the Soul Star Chakra. Although, I feel a more appropriate name would be the Oversoul Chakra. The Soul Star Chakra is our connection to our Higher Consciousness Identity (Higher Self) and the data bank of all knowledge and wisdom gained through our many lifetimes. When this chakra awakens, we begin to establish a bridge between our physical body and our Higher Self. This bridging prepares us for the next stage of consciousness evolution for humanity.

This part of our consciousness is connected to the Hierarchy of Light, the Star Nations, and all the Ascended Beings. Through this chakra, we begin to establish communication with these evolutionary allies. It is our connection to our Greater Divine Purpose and Cosmic Consciousness. The energy is potent, pure, and infinite.

As we begin to interact with this reservoir of Light consciously, every chakra begins to shine brighter as the codes of the Higher Consciousness begin to pour into our body and subtle energy system. The Soul Star updates our entire system from the DNA to the finest particles of light and respatializes the physical and subtle energy architecture into higher geometric harmony and vitality.

Soul Star Activation

Bring your hands to your knees, palms down, and close your eyes, practicing conscious breathing as you tune into your subtle energy and inner realm. Connect with your hara line. As you inhale, lengthen your spine. As you exhale, ground your energy and soften any tension in your body.

Gassho: Bring your hands to prayer position at the heart. Call upon the presence of the Light and feel your vibration begin to rise. Intend to activate the light of your heart, breathe into it, and expand this light. Feel the energy flow into your arms and activate the hands' chakras with the light of your heart.

Reiji-ho: Bring your prayer hands up to touch your thumbs on your forehead. Tune into the center of your skull and activate the Brow Center by intending for it to illuminate. Breathe and expand this light. Intend to activate your inner sight and your connection to the Higher Mind, your Higher Self, star lineages, and guides. Welcome their presence to be with you and ask for their loving consciousness to communicate to your Inner Being.

Bring your hands to the top of your head, palms down, fingertips touching at the center of the head, wrists lightly resting on the side of the head. Tune into the crown chakra and invite it to activate. Tune in to the sensations of your hands as they lightly float just above your head. Breathe into your sensations and invite the energy to flow powerfully as you feel the exchange of light and sensation between your crown and palm chakras. You may sweep and clean the head energetically if you feel called to. Always fill in what you clear with Light.

Begin to peel open the fingers so that the wrists rest on the sides of the head, fingers pointing up like a crown. Slide the hands up so the wrists are at the top of the head. Keep reaching the hands up until you sense that you are holding your Soul Star Chakra. You may feel it light up or even see it in your inner eye. Radiate your love from your hands into the Soul Star Chakra and feel the love there. Make it beautiful and shining bright with the brilliant, golden-white diamond light. Breathe deeply as you connect with the Soul Star and imagine its brilliance and beauty.

Invite the Great Illuminated Ones, the Hierarchy of Light, to work with you. Invite the Star Families of Light to work with you. Welcome your cosmic oversoul consciousness to activate. Breathe into this intention and notice your internal realm.

Begin to bring your hands down to rest on your head, motioning the flow of your Soul Star to connect with your crown chakra. Breathe the energy down through your crown and let it wash through every cell in your body. See each cell and strand of DNA activating with this diamond light.

Open your eyes when you are ready. Know that something deeply transformative has happened. Take this Light out into the World!

Earth Star Chakra: The Super Root

Located six to twelve inches below the feet is the Earth Star Chakra. This is our Super Root connecting us to the Earth's electromagnetic field, grounding our chakras and subtle body. It is a composting system, as we allow any dense energies to be offered to the Earth to be transmuted and cleared from our system. When this center is balanced, we feel connected to our inner power, and we dynamically interact with Gaia in a mutual energy exchange. When it is imbalanced, we may feel dizzy, disconnected, ungrounded, or lightheaded.

The Earth Star Chakra connects us to the life force of Gaia, bringing with it the codes of Inner Earth and the wisdom of the plant, animal, and mineral realms. It is said to contain our karmic imprints, DNA legacy, and information from our past lives on this planet and beyond. It unites us with wisdom from ancient times and our ancestors. It connects us to the evolutionary codes pulsing through the ley lines connecting sacred sites on and off-planet. By establishing a connection to this energy center, we are committed to our life purpose, fully embodied in the NOW moment.

Earth Star Activation

Ground, center, and tune in using Gassho and Reiji-Ho.

Start sitting to get familiar with the chakras of the feet. Bring your hands to the soles of your feet and intend to activate the foot chakras in the soles. Breathe consciously as the chakras in your hands begin to interact with the chakras in your feet. Intend them to connect and trust your sensations. Use your breath and imagination to grow the light and sensitivity in your foot chakras.

Come to standing in mountain pose, *tadasana*, with your feet under your hips. Bring your hands together in prayer at the heart center. Lightly bend the knees and press the edges of the feet into the ground to feel soft length in the legs. Breathe up and down your hara line and sense about six to twelve inches below your feet to your Earth Star Chakra. Intend to connect and know that you are. Trust your sensations.

Breath Light from Source through your hara line and ground it into the Earth Star with each exhale. Let it fractal out like the roots of a tree and spread far and deep into the planet, immersing in her energy. Make it beautiful and powerful. As you do this, imagine that the light is washing all of the dense and stagnant energies you carry down into the roots with gratitude.

Breathing in, drink up the nourishing life force of Gaia and the Earth Kingdoms of Life. Feel the knowledge and wisdom of the Golden Ages of Gaia beginning to fuse with your energy system. Feel your connection to the sacred sites of Earth and beyond. As you exhale, send the energy into the Soul Star Chakra as your entire field blooms like a cosmic fountain pulsating with rainbow light. Let the energy fractal out and create limbs of light that reach out to the higher realms and distant stars.

Breathing in and out, enjoy this exchange of information and light. When you are finished, bring your radiant field closer to you, condensing the light to a comfortable bubble around you. Ground your energy with gratitude, open your eyes, and move throughout your day as a conscious bridge between Heaven and Earth.

Zeal Chakra

The Zeal Chakra, also called the Golden Chalice, Mouth of God, or Well of Dreams, is located at the base of the skull in the occipital ridge region, radiating from the medulla oblongata.

In my research, I found varying information about chakras at the back of the head. In the ancient texts, they speak of the Bindu Chakra and place this energy center at the upper part of the back of the skull. Tradition Chinese Medicine describes the Governing Meridian that runs through this region with several energy points. Maybe the Zeal and Bindu are the same? At the time of this writing, I experience both places activated. Other writings found on the internet describe another structure called the Alta Major

Chakra. I believe all these structures are part of a complex system. Use these descriptions to guide you in your own research. Meditation on this area will reveal what is true and active within you.

The medulla oblongata oversees autonomic nervous system functions like heart and blood vessel function, heartbeat, breathing, and other mostly unconscious functions of our body. The Zeal Chakra connects with the heart's energetic systems, the third eye, crown, and spinal system, including the kundalini. Cosmic Intelligence comes in through the Zeal Chakra to flow through the entire physical and luminous system. We see this idea demonstrated in the movie *The Matrix* when the characters download programs of consciousness from the mainframe computer system into their brains and into the mind of their avatar within the matrix simulation.

As this center activates and regulates, we may begin to experience sensations in this region, including tingling, congestion, headaches, heat, and more. We can do energy work to open the pathway to make room for easier downloading and integration.

Zeal Chakra Activation

Close your eyes and begin to focus on your Inner Being. Bring the hands to the back of the skull, fingertips pointing up towards the crown of the head, wrists resting directly on or lightly over the curve of the occipital ridge.

Take a few moments to tune into the electric and magnetic qualities there. Notice your sensations and inner messaging as you breathe consciously.

Gently use your thumbs to begin to unfurl the petals, the emanations, of the Zeal Chakra. Move the thumbs from the center and outward as if spreading out the energy.

You may have to do some clearing to move out the density. Do this gently with your thumbs. Imagine pure crystalline energy and coding feeding into the emanations of the Zeal Chakra. Imagine that you are receiving evolutionary coding and healing energies from the Divine through the Zeal Chakra. Use your breath and mind to amplify the regenerative feeling.

When you are finished, bring your hands to your lap or heart center. Consciously breathe and notice your sensations. When you are complete, you can open your eyes and enjoy your new connection.

High Heart Chakra

The High Heart Chakra is slightly above the heart center, originating from the thymus gland under a bony protrusion below the center of the clavicle.

This is the Sacred Heart connected to Divine Love. Awakening this High Heart Center brings us out of the old model of conditional love and into the ever-extending grace of unconditional love. Having a healthy High Heart Chakra gives us a healthy immune system as the thymus regulates immune system function. Connecting from this center before we speak ensures compassionate communication and deeper understanding. It brings us into the energy of reconciliation and trust. Connecting with the center before healing sessions opens the pathways of selfless service so that the love of Source can flow through us.

High Heart Activation

Bring your fingers and palpate this region until you find the little bump in the high center of the sternum and begin to lightly tap the bony area with the pad of your fingers. Allow the vibration to echo deep and far into your sternum with the intention of awakening your Sacred Heart. Allow your breath and mind to penetrate deeply into this energy field to invigorate and illuminate this center. Begin to tone or hum, directing the vibrations into this region. With your intention, connect with Divine Love as if the Sun is beginning to rise within your Sacred Heart. Do any clearing that you feel is necessary here. Connect to a sense of gratitude and appreciation for the blessings of your life.

Bring your hands to your lap and feel your sensations. Notice your mood and thoughts. Enjoy your renewed vibration.

ASCENSION LEXICON

I have put together a list of words commonly used in this book and for the topics of awakening, spirituality, and ascension. These are not necessarily defined this way by others but are an excellent way to understand my writings in this book in a more clear and multidimensional way.

-A-

Adamic Form: Original perfected divine human form created for highly developed Light Beings to experience physical creation from within the physical dimension. Fourth Density (4D) body of the New Earth human connecting with oversoul consciousness, higher dimensional beings, and telepathic species.

Agartha: Ancient Inner Earth multi-species civilization with its own sun and ecosystem within the Earth. See *Inner Earth*.

Ain Soph: Kabbalistic term for Source before manifestation into form and translates to "Without Limit" as it is the unlimited creative potential behind all of Creation. Same as "Ineffable" in the Gnostic texts. Can also be written as "Ensof."

Akashic records: Higher-dimensional spiritual records of all experience past, present, and future. Each soul has one. So does each planet and so on.

alchemy: The application of spiritual knowledge to matter to create transformation. This is more commonly known with the Middle Ages' pursuits of turning simple metals into gold. High alchemy being the alchemy of soul/lightbody.

Ancient Egypt: Last golden age of Gaia when many beings held 4th, 5th, and 6th-dimensional consciousness before the descent into lower consciousness (forgetting).

Andromedans: Highly advanced star beings from the Andromeda galaxy assisting humanity's ascension.

Anunnaki: Star beings from the Nibiru system. Sumerian space "gods" who manipulated humanity for personal gain. Now most are in support of humanity's ascension.

apocalypse: 1. Greek word for "unveiling." 2. The dismantling of the mind control matrix and false projections from the controlling forces to reveal to humanity the ugly underbelly and karma of the collective consciousness upon the Earth from this creation cycle which is to be fully reconciled before the planet changes in dimension to Fourth Density New Earth. Not the "end" but a transitionary phase into the next creation cycle.

Archons/Controllers: Term used to describe negatively polarized service-to-self, nonphysical, intelligent beings who siphon negative energy from humanity for their own gain using mind control tactics to keep humanity enslaved through fear and distorted consciousness. The controlling forces behind global institutions. Will be fully dismantled before the shift to New Earth.

Arcturians: Star beings from the constellation of Arcturus assisting Earth with Ascension.

Ascension/ascension: 1. The spiritual maturity process of a soul, moving from an unawakened state of mundane consciousness to multidimensional Source/God-realization described as the movement of the kundalini up the central channel, samadhi, moksha, nirvana, salvation... 2. The movement of Creation into greater states of Glory. 3. The current collective planetary transformation from 3D to 5D consciousness and the New Earth reality.

ascension symptoms: Physical, etheric, mental, and spiritual changes during ascension cycles. Includes headaches, emotional purging, detoxifications symptoms, multidimensional DNA reprogramming, body aches, vivid dreams, and beyond.

Ascended Master: Level of spiritual hierarchy of beings who have ascended in their consciousness enough to no longer need to incarnate in form for spiritual growth but may choose to incarnate to assist the ascension process of a species.

Atman: Divine origin identity, True Self, True Nature, the Witness Consciousness of a lifestream. Same as Brahman. Source Self. Eternally free.

aura: Electromagnetic field of subtle energy that surrounds and pervades the physical body. Contains ever-shifting patterns and geometries of light and vibration that create the template for the physical form.

-B-

biotransducer: organic instrument for transforming energy information for the purpose of manifestation and communication with the universal hologram and divine frequencies. Able to utilize advanced intelligence and spiritual information for the transformation of reality in the human environment.

bodhisattva: Sanskrit term for someone on the path of Buddhahood (ascension) who dedicates their path to the liberation of all beings from cycles of suffering. Able to achieve liberation but delays to assist others in consciousness expansion.

Brahman: The Absolute Reality. Source in impersonal, nonmanifest state. Pure Infinity Existence Consciousness Bliss, *Satchitananda*.

buddhi: the Intellect, reflected consciousness, enlightened consciousness in each person.

buddhic consciousness: enlightened consciousness expressed by *buddhi*, the vehicle for the soul, experienced as profound intuitive insight, unity, and bliss.

-C-

Cabal: Global elite network of negatively polarized service-to-self operatives and organizations working towards complete domination of humanity and planet Earth. See *Archons*.

causal consciousness: the higher mind capacity which utilizes soul memory and intuition to observe and understand manifestation multidimensionally.

centering: Alignment with one's divine nature and inner truth, activating a bridge between Gaia and the Divine through the heart center.

centropy: Regenerative electrification of matter-energy.

chakras: Spiraling transformers of subtle energy with seven primary vortices emanating from the central channel (*sushumna*) which govern our perception of the projected holographic reality and energize our mental and physical processes.

channeling: Opening one's consciousness and vessel as a conduit for subtle energy or other consciousnesses.

Christ: 1. Yeshua ben Joseph (Jesus) in his ascended Lightbody. Forerunner of christ consciousness as part of a divine plan for redemption and restoration of humanity and Earth back to a 4th Density collective. 3. A collective consciousness field that has many emanations and incarnated forms throughout the history of Creation. 4. Title given to one who has achieved consciousness mastery and is "anointed" by Light.

christ consciousness: Also called cosmic consciousness or 5D consciousness. Demonstrated by Jesus of Nazareth in his resurrected 4th Density body.

Christ/Magdalene Lineage: Genetic implantation of higher DNA coding through the offspring of Jesus and Mary. Descendants are worldwide and able to carry a higher light quotient and awaken more easily.

clairaudience: Clear hearing is the ability to hear messages from your Higher Self or spirit beings. This includes hearing the thoughts of other people.

clairgustance: Clear tasting is the ability to receive intuitive information through the sense of taste.

clairesalience: Clear smelling is the ability to intuit information through the sense of smell.

clairvoyance: Clear sight is the ability to perceive information through internal imagery.

clear channeling: Mediumship, or spirit channeling, is the ability to communicate with nonphysical beings and consciousness structures. This can include souls who have passed beyond the veil of physical life or beings that exist in other dimensions.

collective: Representing an entire group, i.e., human collective.

Collective Messiahship: The unification of ascending humanity with the intention of global restoration and ascendency.

cords: Subtle energy attachments that connect us to other beings. Can be negative if developed through limiting beliefs and distorted conditioning.

council: Group of beings joined together with a common focus (i.e., your spiritual council of guides who support your spiritual maturation across lifetimes).

Councils of Light: Groups of advanced spiritual beings that govern the evolution of consciousness and the biological forms of a certain experimental zone to encourage higher states of glory and harmony with the highest being the Universal Council of Light.

-D-

density: 1. Mass per volume. 2. Bandwidth of consciousness reality.

Descension/descension: To go down. The forgetting or falling asleep phases of consciousness. The stepping down of light frequency.

dharma: The noble path of awakening guided through alignment with the Divine through one's True Nature. Exemplified by the life path of beings like Jesus and the Buddha.

The Divine: The frequency emanation that governs and sustains all of Creation across many universes within universes. God Source and the Hosts of Heaven. See *Godhead*.

Divine Androgyny: Harmonic synergy between the divine masculine and divine feminine energetic expressions that results in perfect balance and cohesion.

Divine Creatorship: The birthright of a human to create their life with free-will choice in alignment with their Inner Source.

Divine Feminine: 1. Nurturing creative quality of the Divine 2. Archetypal, spiritual, and psychological ideal of the feminine energetic expression.

Divine Masculine: 1. Administrative quality of the Divine 2. Archetypal, spiritual, and psychological ideal of the masculine energetic expression.

DNA: Genetic blueprint for the development of an organism with both physical and subtle components. Ascended humanity will have 12 fully restored strands.

-E-

Earth Changes: Physical and subtle energetic changes that occur on the planet as it prepares to shift into the next creation cycle. Includes pole shifts, weather changes, seismic and volcanic activity, electromagnetic shifts, and more.

Elohim: First Creation. Creator beings with individual consciousness that work in groups to form Creation. Some created as service-to-all working in unity with Source. Some were created as service-to-self permitted to create in the illusion that they were separate from Source.

empath: Individual who is sensitive to the subtle energy such as thought, and emotional projections of others as they intuitively feel the mental/emotional body of others within their own mental/emotional realm. See *clairsentience*.

End Times: The closing of this current creation cycle where all karma must be balanced, and all shadow revealed so that Earth and spiritually activated humanity can begin the next creation cycle in 4th Density New Earth. See *apocalypse*.

energy: Subtle energy beyond the visible light spectrum ranging from pervasive to neutral to regenerative and life-enhancing. Everything is energy.

energy awareness: Perception of subtle energy in and around one's body.

energy matrix: Geometric organization of subtle frequencies that creates the base structure for the development of form.

entity attachment: Astral debris that has attached itself to a weakened energy system of a host as a source of sustenance and a way to live out "unfinished business." Quite common and easily resolved most of the time by a trained spirit releasement practitioner or energy medicine practitioner.

entropy: Decay and degeneration of matter-energy.

extraterrestrial: From outside of the Earth's biosphere including other planets and universes. There are countless species in our solar system, galaxy, super galaxy, and beyond. Infinite species in infinite realms of creation with many advanced civilizations with histories tracing back trillions of years.

evolution: See *Higher Evolution.*

-F-

false prophets: Teachers and prophets who use spiritual information for service-to-self agendas. Many religious leaders, spiritual teachers, and even those in the ascension community will have their true intentions revealed in the final phases of Ascension.

Family of Light: Physical and nonphysical beings who live their lives in alignment with the Oneness of Creation and the Divine Source. Includes the races of the Star Nations who hold 5D consciousness and higher and the Hierarchy of Light who tend to the many levels of Light Creation.

5D: Consciousness of humans living on the New Earth, can be referred to as christ consciousness or oversoul consciousness.

4D: Awakening stage of ascension bridging mundane consciousness with the New Earth consciousness.

frequency: 1. Rate of vibration measured in hertz (Hz). 2. Higher vibrational rate is likened to positivity and centropy and lower rate towards negativity and entropy.

-G-

Gaia: 1. Sentient Earth 2. Common name for the soul of Earth. Also called Terra.

Galactic Federation of Light: Intergalactic and ultraterrestrial collective of advanced beings who tend to the evolution of consciousness and biological forms throughout the Milky Way. Comprised of advanced scientists, engineers, medical personnel, and other areas of expertise needed to maintain order and balance in the galaxy.

genetic implantation: Seeding of new DNA into the gene pool to evolve a species into higher states of harmony or functionality. Used by the Star Nations and Hierarchy of Light to craft zones of biological experimentation.

gnosis: Direct experience of divine nature through one's own inner being and inner knowing that leads to higher understanding of the nature of the divine reality. See *Knowledge*.

Great Central Sun: Source of all levels of creation in this universe. Brings higher evolutionary coding from Divine Source into other central suns in the universal grid which flow to each solar system evolving each region in accordance with a Divine Plan for Higher Evolution. See *Ishawara.*

Great Divide: The bifurcation of consciousness amongst humanity during the end phases of the planetary ascension process. Includes physical movement across the Earth as humanity moves to be with others of shared consciousness and similar vibration and soul path. Two-world-spit of those who hold negatively polarized, service-to-self consciousness and those of positively polarized, service-to-all consciousness.

Great White Brotherhood: More accurately **Great White Siblinghood**. Ascended Masters, human and non-human, of all gender expressions organized into different orders or councils who tend to the evolution of consciousness and sometimes incarnate to bring new teachings and new energy. Many of these Ascended Masters have aspects of themselves on the planet now to assist the Ascension.

Greys: Extraterrestrial beings from Zeta Reticuli.

God: 1. Supreme Source of Creation 2. Divine Masculine, administrative quality of Godhead, Eternal Mind. See *Ishwara.*

Goddess: 1. Divine Feminine, nurturing, regenerative, creative aspect of the Godhead. 3. Mother God.

Godhead: The Divine Consciousness Source and its various emanations and functions.

Golden Ages: Times of high consciousness and harmony upon the Earth during the Precession of the Equinoxes. (e.g., Avalon, Lemuria)

grounding: The anchoring of one's physical and subtle bodies into the Earth's core through intention, diaphragmatic breathing, and visualization through the Root and Earth Star chakras.

guides: Spiritual beings who assist an incarnated being on their dharmic path towards liberation.

-H-

hara line: Central pillar of light connecting an individual with Gaia and Source.

heart-centered: Action born from inner truth and spiritual ethics through alignment with one's divine nature.

Hierarchy of Light: Various levels of divine consciousness forms, aspects of Source that serve different functions in the evolution of Creation. Ain Soph/Source, Elohim, Archangels, Angelic Realm, Ascended Masters, Ascended Goddesses, Interdimensional Beings, and Restored Humanity in Adamic Form. The Hosts of Heaven.

Higher Evolution: Beyond biological evolution and natural selection, the recoding of experimental zones of the hologram of Creation using divinely encoded frequencies projected through the stellar network which are coordinated by benevolent beings, physical and nonphysical, who serve the evolution of the Divine Plan throughout the Multiverse. Also includes introduction of new genetic expressions into the gene pool, new technologies, and new ideas to be used to evolve the creation into higher order.

Higher Self: 1. The mature part of our consciousness which operates in positively polarized, service-to-all consciousness and is connected to our divine nature. 2. Sovereign self. 3. Harmonic Divine/Human synthesis. 4. Oversoul. 5. Atman.

Holding space: A term used in spiritual growth and self-development circles that means "to hold suffering in an alchemical container of loving awareness so that it may heal."

Holy Spirit Shekinah: The feminine regenerative energy of the Divine. The "presence of God" in the physical dimension. Opening yourself to channel the divine presence begins an alchemical process of light activation that heals and restores all levels of one's being.

-I-

Inner Earth: Ancient and contemporary subterranean civilizations. Many beings went to Inner Earth before the destruction of Lemuria and

Atlantis. See *Agartha*.

intention: Inner resolve to direct one's focus and creative capacity towards a specific goal. *Sankalpa* in Sanskrit.

interdimensional: Existing between dimensions.

intuition: The ability to perceive energy information beyond the five senses before it has become physically manifested in reality. 2. Extrasensory perception.

involution: spiritual consciousness activation that begins as one moves through Ascension and sheds the mind's conditioning.

Ishwara: 1. personal expression of Source. 2. Source in purest manifested form. Commonly called "God" 3. Great Central Sun. 4. Universal Logos.

-J-

Jesus/Yeshua ben Joseph: Master of Light for Earth. Twin flame of Mary Magdalene. Supreme teacher of Divine Love and Ascension. Brought restored DNA and pure Christ Light to the Earth to activate the 4th Density Redemption Plan. Yeshua's cosmic oversoul legacy includes many star systems including the high spiritual schools of Light in the Pleiades and Sirius A and B. His arrival into this dimension of space was the Star of Bethlehem Lightship. His life path was supported by many galactic beings incarnated upon the Earth as well as many extraterrestrials and ultraterrestrial beings. 2. Incarnation of Ascended Master Lord Sananda.

-K-

karma: 1. The sum of a being's actions in this life and in previous existences, both positive and negative actions which influences the soul's path through incarnations.

Knowledge: "Gnosis," divine insight that activates higher consciousness and God-realization. Sanskrit *aparoksha*

kundalini: Serpentine energy originating at the base of the spine that ascends through the sushumna during the awakening process creating ecstatic spiritual expression.

-L-

Lemuria: First advanced human civilization. Often associated with the Pacific Ocean. Destroyed by major flooding and earth changes.

ley lines: Subtle energy pathways that carry evolutionary information across the planetary grid. Also called dragon lines, songlines, telluric lines.

Light: Regenerative divine energy emanations that exist beyond the typical visible light spectrum (Holy Spirit). Different than conventional light from lightbulbs.

Light beings: 1. General term for nonphysical beings of divine origin. See *Family of Light.*

lightbody: 1. subtle body 2. Vital, lower, and higher mind sheaths. 3. Transmigrating soul

Light Conception: The act of conceiving a child directly from the spiritual realms without the need of sperm from a physical being.

Light language: 1. Language spoken through connection to the Divine Presence. Activates multidimensional healing and powerful internal experiences with healing frequencies. Gift of the Holy Spirit, the regenerative creative frequency that quickens and restores all levels of Life. Can be self-initiated or pushed through from the Higher Self and the Divine.

Light Seed: Higher-dimensional, light-encoded genetic material used for Light Conception and altering the genetic composition of a species. Aka *Immaculate Conception.*

Lightship/lightship: Divine craft made by one individual's lightbody/merkaba or a merged merkaba from more than one being for the purpose of interdimensional travel through space-time, stargates, and higher light realms.

Love: Beyond egoic love, unconditional love that is naturally expressed when one develops love for the divine and a service-to-all intention. *Agape* love.

lokas: Sanskrit word for the planes of existence.

loosh: energy of suffering and death harvested by negative human, extraterrestrial, and interdimensional beings which is used to fuel nefarious agendas.

Lyrans: Star beings from the constellation of Lyra. Most commonly known race is the feline beings. First humanoid race in the Milky Way. Original 144,000 oversoul starseeds to bring the human species to Earth.

-M-

magic(k): Use of universal, natural law, and intention to manifest. Can be either service-to-self (dark) or service-to-all (light).

manifestation: The materialization of intention into form.

mantra: Holy names and phrases repeatedly spoken or thought which generate divine thoughtforms to reprogram the physical, etheric, and mental bodies opening one's consciousness to higher perception, divine insight, and union with the Divine. Use of mantra repatterns the DNA, clearing distortion and debris and reprogramming it into higher order and functionality for the projection of divine consciousness light.

Mary Magdalene: Twin Flame and Divine Partner of Jesus. Ancient Egyptian Priestess. High initiate from the Pleiades, Venus, and other high consciousness realms. Arrived at Earth with Yeshua in the Star of Bethlehem Lightship. Gave birth to the offspring of Jesus. This lineage is spread throughout the world.

maya: Illusion. Projecting and veiling power of Source. All that has form and name which tests our ability to see the all-pervasive divine consciousness that supports all manifestations.

meditation: Conscious focusing of the mind on a single object.

merkaba: Divine light vehicle in the auric field that gives one the ability to travel to the higher light realms. Introduced back to humanity through Elijah.

Michael: Archangel who protects and defends all levels of Creation and biological life.

mindfulness: The practice of bringing our life's gross and subtle manifestations into the light of our awareness to observe life in nonduality. Nondual awareness is the ability to see beyond the illusion of duality and see with the eyes of loving awareness.

Mother Mary: Cosmic divine being, a Master soul, who incarnated to give birth to Jesus. High priestess of Ancient Egypt and master teacher of the cosmic priestess arts.

multidimensional: Existing in multiple planes of consciousness, i.e., physical, etheric, mental, and various spiritual dimensions.

Multiverse/multiverse: Universes within universes creating the totality of Creation. What Jesus spoke of when he referred to his "Father's house with many mansions."

-N-

nadis: Pathways of subtle energy in the body. There are said to be 72,0000 that weave in and around the physical body.

New Earth: 1. Higher density light spectrum reality of the ascended Earth. 2. Kingdom of Heaven on Earth.

nirvanic consciousness: liberated consciousness which has transcended suffering, limited egoic identity, and karmic cycles.

-O-

Orion: Constellation with ancient intelligent races with varying levels of consciousness and ranges of polarity. Factions of Reptilian and humanoid beings from Orion fought against Lyrans in the long galactic war.

oversoul: Higher consciousness identity of a soul. Where your individual soul comes from. Collective consciousness of myriad life streams and incarnations. 4th Density/5D Self.

-P-

past life regression: Form of hypnosis or shamanic journeying that evokes information from a client's subconscious mind from previous lifetimes.

Pleiadians: Star beings from the constellation of Pleiades, a highly advanced light consciousness school in our great universe. Cousins of humanity. They implanted upgraded DNA in humanity to open our spiritual connection.

prayer: Approach to the Divine through thought or word which opens the pathways for the living Light to infuse the one who is praying with love and divine insight.

priest: Male devotee of the Divine in service to the illumination of collective consciousness and the ascension of humanity. Administers the will and knowledge of the divine upon the Earth as well as the regenerative, healing presence of the divine feminine.

priestess: Female devotee of the Divine. Often connected to the Goddess. Embodies the wisdom of the divine feminine mothering principle of the Godhead. Matures consciousness in the community into higher states of creativity, sensuality, and grace.

psychic: One who has extrasensory perception. See *intuition*.

pyramids: Sacred architectural sites around the Earth built by various extraterrestrial and ultraterrestrial beings connecting the pathways of vital energy of the Earth with the universal energy grid for the reprogramming of life upon planet Earth. Act as broadcast and receiving systems for information used for planetary evolution.

Prakriti: Manifested reality, transactional reality as opposed to Absolute Reality, maya.

Purusha: Indwelling witness of Creation, Absolute Reality, Brahman, Pure Consciousness. Source Consciousness.

-Q-

quantum: Dealing with the holographic reality and fabric of Consciousness and creation.

quantum consciousness: Holographic consciousness connecting to the matrix of Creation with the ability to focus across time and space through nonlocality and consciousness projection.

quantum healing: Rapid, multidimensional healing that works at the cellular and subtle levels to bring the body's systems into homeostasis. Can be done through psychic processes, shamanic and energy medicine practices, hypnosis, quantum healing technology, star technology, and divine emanations. This is the medicine of New Earth.

quantum mysticism: Emerging evolutionary synthesis between science, metaphysics, and spirituality used to understand Consciousness and the laws that govern Creation.

Qumran: Ancient, multigenerational esoteric Essene community by the Dead Sea in present-day Israel that lived in complete recognition of the Divine through the study and embodiment of divine mystery teachings. Secretive community with advanced star knowledge and superhuman spiritual abilities. Traded knowledge with other global mystery schools and was home and school to Yeshua, Jesus of Nazareth. Yeshua's children studied here as well.

-R-

Reiki: 1. Japanese word meaning spiritual intelligence life force. 2. Intelligently-encoded, divine, redemptive, and regenerative energy from Source. 3. A gift of the Holy Spirit.

Redemption Plan: Cosmic and galactic initiative to restore humanity and Earth back to 4th Density as in the times of Lemuria. Includes genetic implantation, restoration of planetary grid, and operatives incarnating as human to bring new ideas and technologies, broadcasting intelligent and spiritual coding into the biofield of Earth and humanity, and more.

Reptilians: Reptilian humanoid star beings who have had a "negative" influence on Earth who have mostly evolved to positive polarity. Humans have reptilian DNA that gives us our ego mind to assist our perseverance in evolving.

reincarnation: The act of being born again into a new lifestream for the purpose of spiritual growth.

resonance: In spiritual terms, harmonic, synchronous vibrations between two or more objects.

Raphael: Archangel who administers to healing.

-S-

sacred sexuality: Alchemical sexual expression with the intention of uniting with the divine through one's own erotic spiritual nature. Can be practiced alone or with a partner(s).

sacred sites: Holy power spots spread across the planet that form a web of vortex points for subtle energy pathways of the Earth.

samsara: 1. Wheel of Karma 2. rounds and rounds of incarnations on the path of Ascension 3. Suffering mind. 4. Cycles of suffering.

samskaras: Grooves in the mind that create reactive emotions forming our biases, habits, and tendencies. Can be seen as negative or positive.

Self: Divine Self as opposed to the egoic self which is trapped in worldly conditioning.

sentience: The ability to feel, be conscious, or have one's own subjective experience.

service-to-all: Positively polarized, dedicated intention, thought, and action towards the Greater Good and Higher Love as an extension of one's True Self.

service-to-self: Negatively polarized, gives power to false self, ego. Can seem "positive" as intentions can be different than presentation.

sin: Intention, thought, and action that goes against one's inner light that causes an immediate depletion of life force and positive vibration. Serves the egoic self. There is no judgment for this from higher realms. All is for learning and growth. 2. Fear-based judgment system created by religion which connects to belief systems that limit the indwelling of spiritual light by creating perpetual states of fear, shame, and guilt. 3. The fundamental illusion of separation from Source.

Sirians: Star beings from the region of the Sirius A and Sirius B binary star system who have a long, positive history with humanity and are assisting Earth now.

Solaris: Central sun and stargate of our solar system which emanates supraliminal coding for the evolution of the myriad lifeforms in our solar system.

soul: 1. Subtle bodies which transmigrate from one life to the next. See *lightbody.*

spiritual partnership: A relationship that is supported by the desire to assist one another in awakening and healing.

soul contracts: Pre-designed plan and agreements before incarnating for the balancing of karma to propel the path of liberation and ascension. Includes soul agreements between individual souls to play out certain catalyst roles.

soul purpose: Divine intention for a soul for its incarnation encompassing the themes to be explored and lessons to be learned throughout a lifestream. Generally, a soul's purpose is to awaken to Higher Love and Divine Truth.

sovereign: natural consciousness state of the Atman/Self/Inner Source. Human beings embody and reclaim sovereignty through involution and higher consciousness evolution. Able to have agency in all areas of life. Self-regulated. Self-governed.

stargate: Portal used for transportation between long distances and different dimensions.

Star Nations: Space-traveling intelligent species, some positive, some negative, some neutral in relation to humanity and the Earth.

starseeds: Visitors from other schools in the multiverse who have volunteered to live a human life to assist the Ascension of Gaia and humanity. Many of which have experienced ascension mastery in other lifetimes. The best ascension masters from the universe are here on the planet or around the planet in crafts at this time.

substratum: 1. **Foundational,** base material 2. Source/Brahman/Atman/Pure Consciousness.

superluminal: 1. faster than light

synchronicity: The meeting of two or more seemingly unrelated events or objects that come together in a meaningful way that could even be perceived as divinely coordinated.

-T-

timelines: Pathways of probable events. Infinite potentials and realities fractal out and converge at particular junction points in "time" where choice points exist for the next fractal offshoots of timeline potentials. We are currently moving with multiple timeline potentials for Ascension events that lead to one inevitable event, 4th/5th Density New Earth. Timelines are constantly in flux depending on personal moment-to-moment choices from individuals or the collective meaning the future is never "fixed" but is always in flux. This is the reason why some psychics see different potential probabilities playing out in the future.

3D: Standard human consciousness in its unawakened state, fear/duality-based consciousness which is heavily programmed and hypnotized by the false matrix, the conditioning of the world, and the mind control techniques from the Archons.

Elders: Highest divine council. Progenitors of all cultures in the multiverse.

Twin Flames: Emanations of the same oversoul who assist one another in Ascension. Often uniting at the end of karmic cycles to serve Consciousness. Most commonly thought of as two people in Divine Partnership, but there can be more.

-U-V-W-Y-

Unified Field: The hologram of Creation, the Quantum Field, where all energies and manifestations arise from connecting all through Source Consciousness.

ultraterrestrial: Beings from beyond the physical plane, higher density beings in higher density forms.

vibration: The invisible, subtle layers of matter that form the basic templates for physical reality through repetitive oscillation.

Wisdom: Insight into the Divine Mysteries of Creation and the Godhead that connects us with higher states of divine love and divine grace. See *Knowledge, gnosis.*

walk-in: Exchange of souls during an incarnation. Typically occurs when the original soul consciousness assigned to the body can no longer continue an incarnation from trauma or some other way of vital depletion. A fresh soul consciousness is brought in to accomplish a certain task. Frequently used to bring highly developed galactic beings into the Earth for mission-oriented tasks.

Yeshua ben Joseph: See *Jesus* and *Christ*.

Recommended Reading

The Three Waves of Volunteers and The New Earth by Dolores Cannon
They Walked with Jesus by Dolores Cannon
Jesus and the Essenes by Dolores Cannon
Between Death and Life by Dolores Cannon
Keepers of The Garden by Dolores Cannon
Five Lives Remembered by Dolores Cannon
Return of the Bird Tribes by Ken Carey
Anna: Grandmother of Jesus by Claire Heartsong
Light on Life by B.K.S. Iyengar
The Yoga Sutras of Patanjali (many translations available)
Living Buddha, Living Christ by Thich Nhat Hahn
Reconciliation: Healing the Inner Child by Thich Nhat Hahn
Peace is Every Step by Thich Nhat Hahn
The Path of Energy by Dr. Synthia Andrews
The Seat of the Soul by Gary Zukav
The Book of Knowing and Worth by Paul Selig
The Diamond in Your Pocket by Gangaji
The Magdalen Manuscript: The Alchemies of Horus & the Sex Magic of Isis by Tom Kenyon and Judi Sion
The Kybalion by Three Initiates
Aparokshanubhuti by Adi Shankara
The Upanishads
The Bhagavad Gita
Drig Drishya Viveka
The Keys of Enoch by J.J. Hurtak
Pistis Sophia translated by J.J. Hurtak
The Secret Doctrine by H.P. Blavatsky
Etheric Double by A.E. Powell
The Causal Body and the Ego by A.E. Powell
Regression: Past-life Therapy for Here and Now by Samuel Sagan
Entity Possession: Freeing the Energy Body of Negative Influences by Samuel Sagan

THE ILLUMINATION CODEX

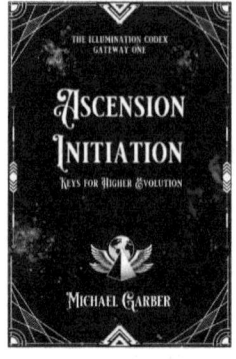

THE ILLUMINATION CODEX
GATEWAY ONE

ASCENSION INITIATION
KEYS FOR HIGHER EVOLUTION

MICHAEL GARBER

THE ILLUMINATION CODEX
GATEWAY TWO PART ONE

QUANTUM ORIGINS
KEYS FOR ANCIENT COSMOLOGY

MICHAEL GARBER

THE ILLUMINATION CODEX
GATEWAY TWO PART TWO

COSMIC CHRIST TRANSMISSIONS
THE MINISTRY OF LIGHT

MICHAEL GARBER

THE ILLUMINATION CODEX
GATEWAY FOUR

CHAKRA YOGA DISCOURSE
KEYS FOR HIGHER CONSCIOUSNESS

MICHAEL GARBER

THE ILLUMINATION CODEX
GATEWAY TWO PART THREE

NEW EARTH TRANSMISSIONS
FUTURE TIMELINES OF GAIA

MICHAEL GARBER

THE ILLUMINATION CODEX
GATEWAY THREE

PATH OF AWAKENING
KEYS FOR TRANSFIGURATION

MICHAEL GARBER

THE ILLUMINATION CODEX
GATEWAY FIVE

LAYING OF HANDS
REIKI & BEYOND

MICHAEL GARBER

WWW.NEWEARTHASCENDING.ORG

Support Our Initiatives

Ron and I have dedicated our lives to supporting this Grand Transition. We stand alongside all of you as humanity awakens to its True Nature and becomes a People of Light in the heavenly reality of New Earth.

New Earth Ascending is dedicated to assisting people to realize their divinity and manifest that truth in every aspect of their life. For more information about New Earth Ascending or to contact Michael, please scan the QR code below for a list of resources and links, or visit *www.newearthascending.org*. Be sure to check out our courses including the Illuminated Quantum Healing practitioner course.

New Earth Ascending is a registered 508 (c)(1)(a) Self-Supported Non-profit Church Ministry with a global outreach. We greatly appreciate your support as we create new systems, communities, and schools for the development of the New Earth civilization. If you would like to make a tax-deductible donation to support our mission, please go to:

https://donorbox.org/donationtonewearthascending

Scan with a smart device camera for more information including websites, social media, and more! Bless us all!

www.ingramcontent.com/pod-product-compliance
Lightning Source LLC
Chambersburg PA
CBHW071405120626
46546CB00002B/817